RIPENING HAY

RIPENING HAY

ALEX HAY

PARTRIDGE PRESS

LONDON · NEW YORK · TORONTO · SYDNEY · AUCKLAND

TRANSWORLD PUBLISHERS LTD
61–63 Uxbridge Road, London W5 5SA

TRANSWORLD PUBLISHERS (AUSTRALIA) PTY LTD
15–23 Helles Avenue, Moorebank, NSW 2170

TRANSWORLD PUBLISHERS (NZ) LTD
Cnr Moselle and Waipareira Aves,
Henderson, Auckland

Published 1989 by Partridge Press
a division of Transworld Publishers Ltd
Copyright © Alex Hay 1989

British Library Cataloguing in Publication Data
Hay, Alex, *1933–*
Ripening hay.
1. Golf – Biographies
I. Title
796.352′092′4

ISBN 1–85225–091–7

Printed in Great Britain
by Mackays of Chatham PLC, Chatham, Kent

Picture credits
Photos Ltd p.1 (bottom); H W Neale p.2 (top); Fred Spencer
p.2 (bottom); Doug McKenzie p.3 (top); Sports Photo-Graphics
p.3 (bottom), p.6 (bottom); Walter Dirks p.8

To Ann – for her tolerance.

CONTENTS

1 Musselburgh   9
2 Starting work – the Stock Exchange and Ben Sayers   16
3 The Silver Cup   22
4 Chris Hanlon   25
5 Ill-gotten gains   29
6 Fiery the caddie   31
7 Various visits to Muirfield   36
8 Ancient clubmaking skills in modern times   43
9 National Service   47
10 Bill Shankland, 'the Boss'   53
11 Johnny Riscoe, dog-lover   61
12 My own job – East Herts   66
13 The 'customer's shot'   73
14 My first Assistant   76
15 Tournament golf – and friends   79
16 The final tournament   83
17 Dunham Forest   87
18 Le Touquet   94
19 Bastille Night   97
20 The Casino   99
21 Harry Bentley   101
22 Ashridge – Secretary and guests   103

23	Henry Cotton	106
24	Ashridge – front runner	108
25	Have clubs, will travel	109
	Portugal and Spain	109
	Florida	111
	South Africa	115
	California	118
26	All at sea	124
27	Modelling	128
28	Summer school	133
29	Writing and drawing	139
30	After dinner	142
31	Jimmy Tarbuck	148
32	Jack Hennessy	151
33	Woburn and Peter Alliss	153
34	Woburn and Greg Norman	156
35	Woburn and Seve Ballesteros	161
36	Woburn and Gary Player	169
37	Company days	173
38	The Ryder Cup	175
39	BBC Television	178
40	A trilogy of cars	185
41	Doctors	190
42	Commenting abroad	195
43	The team	199
44	Learning the trade	205
45	Clive	211
46	My mistake	215
47	Back to the office	220

1

MUSSELBURGH

Unlike most of the youngsters who took up golf in the town of Musselburgh, I was one who did not come from a golfing family. Not only that: possibly because I was born two miles away in Portobello, I did not begin until the age of fifteen which, by Scottish standards, is considered 'a bit too late to do any good.' What's more, the manner in which I took to the game – which, from the moment I started, became a way of life – could be described as slightly unusual.

Fortunately in our house the kitchen cupboard was the resting-place of an old canvas golf bag which contained a few ancient hickory-shafted clubs, remnants of my father's frustrated and short-lived introduction to the game over Portobello Links between shifts as a tram-car driver. Those clubs which had actually survived his few efforts had been left to end their days in darkness, and it was from there that I selected a rusting mid-iron. Not to hit golf balls, but to mow the lawn.

By lawn I mean a ten by twenty yard patch of grass, cornered by four metal clothes-poles, its centrepiece a wartime Anderson air raid shelter into which three families had crowded on the night of the first air raid on the nearby Leith Docks and never again. Nothing Adolf Hitler could fling at us could be so miserable as sitting all night on a cold concrete ledge, our feet dangling into the pit in the centre, looking at each other through the misted-up windows of Mickey Mouse gas masks, waiting for the bombs and the gas to arrive. Few remained until the all clear, but went home, disillusioned.

From that night the shelter became the storage area for all unused household items with the fortunate exception of the clubs, and the grass and weeds grew over and around it uninterrupted until they became totally unmanageable; then the family would take turns at trying to push a vintage Ransomes sidewheel lawnmower over it.

An agonizing task avoided by the use of an inexhaustible supply of excuses. Even school homework was preferred.

Having been informed by Mother, in no uncertain manner, that I would be cutting the grass on the following Saturday afternoon I applied quantities of oil to the rusting works in the hope of easing my task, but within only a few minutes of pushing and pulling the dilapidated piece of machinery I had cleared little or no greenery and was already exhausted.

It was then, as I groped around in the kitchen cupboard in search of some shears we might have borrowed from a neighbour and failed to return, that I spotted the golf clubs.

Within minutes I had developed what I would now describe as a fairly upright swing-plane, from which well-cocked wrists unleashed the clubhead at great speed through the base of the arc. I had in fact discovered the ultimate grass-cutter.

In no time at all I was able to decimate areas of grass, dock leaves and nettles, so that they were reduced to what resembled a finely scythed meadow. Sadly, of course, there was the odd incident which resulted in our next-door neighbour's washing being covered in earth and sod. This did not go unnoticed by Mrs Paterson, who was becoming angrier by the minute at the Hay family's latest means of neighbourly disruption, but more fortunately by her husband John, an ex-Chief Engineer in the Merchant Navy who, probably because he had survived being sunk by three different submarines and spent much of his war in open boats in the North Atlantic and had since become a golfing fanatic, had gained a degree of patience and acceptance. Whether it had been the frustration of mastering golf, which we were all convinced had given John more sleepless nights than Admiral Doenitz, and meant he understood the problems I was having with my swing that persuaded him to ignore his wife's plea to stop me, I know not, but he allowed me to continue whilst he studied my progress from behind their curtains.

Finally, one violent follow-through, intended to remove a well-rooted thistle, found my mid-iron tangled in Mrs Paterson's black-market silk stockings, shattering the blobs of ladder-stopping nail varnish in these, the last pair to survive a burning tanker that went down in minutes, followed by three weeks in an open lifeboat.

This was the last straw, and my new-found golf career seemed destined to a sudden end.

'What are you going to tell him?' screamed Mrs Paterson as she and I unwound her precious cargo from the rusting clubhead and splintered shaft. 'I'm going to tell him to leave his hit till later in

the downswing!' John had now found himself a new golfing partner and I had found a new grass-cutting assistant.

The rest of the afternoon was spent productively, Mrs Paterson stitching and varnishing Musselburgh's only pair of United States fully fashioned seamed stockings, the envy of all the ladies at Bridge Street Church on Sunday mornings, and admired by all the elders (Mrs Paterson had lovely legs), whilst John and I were hard at work perfecting my golf swing. By going slowly back, then starting down patiently, leaving the acceleration till the very last moment, the cuts of grass were longer, and the divots, as we ran out of grass, became less frequent.

My father, an immaculate man who was following his own ambitions and was now a dance-band leader, returned from his weekly visit to the hairdresser prior to donning the white tie and tails which were his Saturday night uniform and leaving for work. He was naturally overjoyed that the garden, compared to its previous state, now looked like Hampden Park, but more important he was delighted that I was being encouraged to take up golf. What's more, by coincidence Father had, just five minutes earlier, been in conversation in the barber's shop with a gentleman by the name of

11

John Aitken who had spent his life as a professional golfer and teacher at no less a club than Wentworth, and who had now retired to live out his days in Musselburgh.

My father, John Paterson, and I left immediately for the barber's shop, where I was introduced as the most natural swinger my neighbour had ever seen, from which recommendation John Aitken undertook to coach me, and under his patient guidance I learned the basics of the golf swing and was introduced to the most wonderful game there is. From him I learned of the traditions of the game and how golf professionals, even in those days when most were not allowed into clubhouses, still had a dignity that was an example to those who were.

Musselburgh possesses no fewer than three courses: Monktonhall, the Royal Musselburgh, which has the oldest trophies in golf in its vaults and for whom I became one of the junior members in their club team, and the nine-hole Old Links Course, which happens to be the oldest golf course left in the world. Strangely enough, although both John Aitken and I lived only a very short distance from Monktonhall Golf Club it was to the Old Links that 'Mr Aitken' and I would go by bus when my form was lost. This was because of a slight rivalry that existed between him and another who had also retired and had been installed at Monktonhall as the Professional. He was Jack White, not only a past Open Champion but the former Senior Professional at Sunningdale, and who made no bones about pointing out to all and sundry that John Aitken had only been an Assistant at neighbouring Wentworth. Mr Aitken therefore preferred to give his few lessons on the Links, inconvenient though it was in those days when few owned cars.

Those who have played the Old Links, where Open Championships were played and which was the home of the very first Champion, Willie Park, where the Foreman's pub is situated at the Levenhall end with all its historic tales, will know only too well that the course is also the home of the Edinburgh Race Course.

Although horseracing has taken place there for centuries, since it was discovered that linksland turf, with its excellent drainage, provides one of the finest surfaces for the sport, it unfortunately became necessary in more recent times to fence the track fully, which obviously affected the golf course. Later, when a longer straight was added, the famous 'Foreman's' hole was dissected, and it became a case of driving over the race track with great accuracy, sufficiently to the right to gain an extremely narrow strip of that which was the fairway, whilst avoiding the tram-cars that rattled from Musselburgh to Edinburgh every ten minutes (except when it was raining, when they came hourly). Today the National Hunt has persuaded those with no sense of golfing tradition to build yet another track inside that of the 'flat' and has virtually destroyed what should have been preserved for as long as golf is played.

However, it was up against those railings that a good deal of my personal tuition time was spent and where I learned a lesson that I have used all of my life, and one which, leaping forward to the present, I see the world's greatest player of golf, Seve Ballesteros, exercise. Like every youngster, particularly one who was never too big in stature, nor in possession of great strength, the desire to hit the ball as far as possible regularly caused the swing to break up.

'But it's my driving that's gone off,' I would plead as Mr Aitken would hand me my old hickory niblick. Pitching balls, when I wanted desperately to cure the slice or the diving hook of my tee shots, was eating into the valuable minutes of my five-shilling session. But the cure was always the same, for swinging, as Seve says today, is all about tempo.

Mr Aitken would stand me on the other side of the five-foot-high race-track rail and make me lob the ball, using my wrists, as near to slow motion as I could, so that total feel of the clubhead became the controlling factor. We only ever owned a box of six balls in those days, so, when all had been lobbed successfully over the rail from the track onto the course, we would retrieve them and move closer.

'Please let me show you my poor drives.'

'One more row of balls, please,' was always the reply.

By the time the lesson was nearly over, my left shoulder would be within a few feet of the railing (which, at five feet, was considerably above me too) and the subtle timing of the wrists, with the easy movement from the legs, which is essential yet often neglected in short pitching shots, plus a laid-open blade, would have the six balls rising nearly vertically up and over the rail, landing like soft-poached eggs on that beautiful turf of the 9th green.

'Now you can show me your poor drive,' he would say, teeing up just one ball, and every time the result was the same. Straight and true – the lesson had been learned: if the clubhead doesn't do the work, then nothing works!

To the young having an Open Champion in our midst was a great thrill, and it was with eager anticipation we made our first visit to Jack White's shop, for it was there you would search the corners for secondhand bargains. We would browse amongst the bits and pieces whilst he totally ignored us, which we assumed was one of the privileges that went with being Open Champion.

My massive but short-lived support for his services came to

an end when, having spent several hours over a period of weeks, picking it up, waggling it about, picturing the great shots I would hit with it, and dreading someone else would have it before me, I finally invested all of my savings, a little over one pound, on my first steel-shafted club.

At the first hole, after a good drive with my hickory-shafted brassie/driver down that lovely cascading opening fairway at Monktonhall, what luck, just the yardage left for a steel-shafted no. 4 iron. The swing was sweet and true, then there was a strange feel when I hit the ball. Surely this was not the painful experience some elder members who, shunning progress by clinging to their hickories, said we would have if we converted from the sweet-feeling wood shafts to these newfangled lumps of iron.

It wasn't! My ball went one way and my clubhead the other. The shaft had snapped where it joined the head.

Back I went up the fairway to the shop in a state of total depression. Surely an Open Champion, late of Sunningdale, would give me my money back. Not a hope.

'It'll cost you 3s 6d to repair!'

Not only did it cost 3s 6d, it took four weeks to complete the job. Nevertheless the pain was over and I had my club again; the high cost of repair was because he 'had bound the shaft inside the head with copper wire', which, even to my non-mechanical brain, seemed like quite an achievement.

The following Saturday morning (Musselburgh was wisely encouraging youngsters to play in competitions) my drive at the first hole was perfect, even with the pressures of a Monthly Medal upon me. Almost from the same spot where a month ago my clubhead flew off, I played my newly repaired steel-shafted no. 4 iron. This time the head flew even further. This time I didn't go back to the former Open Champion, I just collected the head, put it in the bag, left the course and went home.

My elder brother, Bill, who was an apprentice marine engineer with Brown Brothers in Leith took my no. 4 iron to where they built the steering gear for the Queen Mary and Queen Elizabeth, drilled a hole through the socket and riveted my no 4. iron together. Now I had a steel-shafted club and I had learned a valuable lesson that I hope I have carried through my career as a club professional and teacher of many young golfers, that there has to be trust between pro and pupil, if either is to succeed.

It would be wrong to write of Musselburgh and our young days just after the Second World War without mentioning one of today's greatest living golf historians, George Colville, now in his nineties, who did so much for the town's young golfers, correcting us when our etiquette was not up to standard, teaching us, playing with us (he still plays with his own grandchildren and over the same old course) that he became a part of all of our lives.

We used to sit by the old clubhouse and listen to tales of how old George, as a schoolboy in short trousers, would set off to school from his home just behind the Foreman's Inn, and there would be Willie Park relentlessly practising his putting: Willie, the greatest putter of his time, who preached 'that a man who can putt is a match for anyone'. At night, from his bedroom window, George would peer out into the twilight and there would be Willie Park, a white handkerchief stuffed into the hole to help sight it, still working. George even swears that he saw him practising late into the night with a burning candle stood up behind the hole, knocking in those vital short ones.

To this day, George, who spent his working life with the local authorities, claims his saddest moment was when the relatives of the ageing Willie Park came and begged him to find a space in Musselburgh's Poor House. This, difficult though it was (for in those days that was a very busy establishment), he managed to do, and was rewarded by being given a box of the legendary Willie Park hand-forged putter-heads which he might possibly sell. George still has them.

It was over those ancient links that I had one of my proudest achievements, when I won the Musselburgh Boy's Championship and received the silver medal.

I remember vividly requiring two 3s to win. I got the par 3 at the 17th (you played the nine holes twice), and then I had to make a birdie at the par 4 closing hole. I hit a cracking drive with my old brassie/driver that made the green. Two putts and the title was mine.

Many years later, when *en route* to St Andrews to play in the Centenary Open, I stopped off at the Old Links for a spot of practice. I emptied out my bag of sparkling practice balls and from that same 18th tee, using my *de luxe* model driver I pounded them all over the hill towards the green. Not one of the balls got within twenty-five yards of it.

2

STARTING WORK –
THE STOCK EXCHANGE AND
BEN SAYERS

Strangely enough, although I feel I have been involved in professional golf all my life, this is not so, for I actually did not set
out to be a professional player – something I subsequently proved
might well have been the correct decision. I started my working life
by joining a stockbroking office in George Street in Edinburgh.

I hasten to add that I did not join the Stock Exchange
because of any flair for making money, another fact I have
subsequently proved correct, but because it was commonly known
that the Edinburgh Stock Exchange was a hotbed of golfers. The
Exchange was housed in a superb red stone building on the north-
west corner of St Andrew's Square and was later demolished to be
replaced by one of those concrete monstrosities about which Prince
Charles openly expresses opinion, and which (and this would be to
His Royal Highness's delight) was the subject of a crash, not of the
Wall Street variety; it simply fell in like a pack of cards. As a result
the Edinburgh Stock Exchange is now in Glasgow.

More important to me, stockbroking was the only office job in
those days that worked a five-day week. The brokers could even
come to work on a Friday dressed in sports jackets and flannels
rather than suits, so that an early getaway could take place immediately upon close of trading on Friday afternoons. George Street, and
most streets around St Andrew's Square fairly rang with the rattling
of golf-clubheads as the business minds of Scotland's capital rushed,
with their clubs on their shoulders, to the various bus stops of the St
Andrew's Square terminal. The favourite and busiest of these were
sited on the north side, within only a few yards of the Exchange

16

building, the buses standing in a row with their destinations clearly marked, like a golfing tourist guide:

MUSSELBURGH: LONGNIDDRY: ABERLADY:
GULLANE: NORTH BERWICK: DUNBAR.

So busy were those buses on a Friday that anyone finishing after 4.00 p.m. would probably have to stand in the aisle, clutching his clubs to him for the entire journey along that golfing coastline.

I thoroughly enjoyed my spell working in Edinburgh and studied the workings of the Stock Exchange at Herriot Watt College. It is quite likely that I would have continued in that way of life but for the unfortunate and untimely death of my employer, which occurred just a few months before I was due to be called up for National Military Service.

I was assured by the Secretary of the Stock Exchange that many of the city's brokers were extremely interested in employing me, and if I would stay on and help redistribute all of my present office's clients to other brokers he would guarantee me the position of my choice. I fulfilled my part of the bargain and duly turned up at his office on the top floor of the Exchange. It only took a few phone calls to establish that, with my call-up imminent, I was unemployable, and much to the Secretary's genuine disappointment I was on the dole.

The one consolation of being on what the locals called 'the Broo' was that the Bureau was across the road from the Old Course, so I didn't have far to go to collect my fifteen shillings each week, and it was on my way back to the course that my old friend Mr Aitken found me. He was concerned at my plight and suggested that I should consider making the game of golf my life by turning professional.

There was no doubt in those days that the only place to go as an Assistant Professional was south to England, which is what Mr Aitken was urging me to do, but first I would have to possess something other than the love of golf to persuade a Club Professional to hire me. What was needed was some clubmaking skill, for, in those days, the repairing of clubs was an essential part of the Professional's service to his members.

The only place to gain such training was in the factory of the renowned Ben Sayers, some twenty miles along the coast from Musselburgh. When I suggested to Mr Aitken that no one would consider me, as I was only weeks away from enlistment, I was informed that Ben Sayers was an important exporter, which meant that apprentices could defer call-up until the completion of their training. Next day I knocked on the door of Ben Sayers' office, explained to him my predicament, and within the hour started my apprenticeship.

Looking back on those days when British clubmakers ruled the roost, I am saddened when I think 'Where have they all gone?'. Was it their stubborn determination to stick to traditional manufacturing methods that allowed the American to take over? Could it have been the shortage of finance, or the ridiculous tax situation? Or was it the complacency that seemed to be the British disease in the sixties? Strangely enough the Japanese at that time were no threat at all, though they certainly are today: then they produced absolute garbage which offered no opposition. The only competitors were on the other side of the Atlantic, and we should have been able to compete.

The result was that the great names like Forgan of St Andrews, Nicol of Leven, Gibson of Kinghorn, Scott of Ely, St Andrews Golf Company, Gradidge, the Spalding factories, and so many others, disappeared. Even John Letters of Glasgow was gobbled up by Dunlop, who later disgorged it, thankfully back into the hands of the Letters family, who still make superb clubs.

Ben Sayers, to whom I owe so much, have, thanks to takeovers and modern commercial management, weathered the storm and are still going strong. Whether this would be the case had they stuck to the stubborn traditional principles which existed when I was there I doubt very much.

One of the great boasts then was that our clubs were 'Hand Forged', which common sense will tell you is one way of never finishing up with a matched set of clubs. We used to sneer at John Letters' drop-forged clubheads, claiming the steel to be so soft that, unlike our hardened steel models that kept their shine for generations, they dented and chipped just by rubbing together. The fact that each club in the set matched the other, and that professionals who used them claimed a much sweeter feel, did not deter Ben Sayers one bit.

The fact that our clubs were in such demand around the world – a fact which was keeping me out of the forces – was seen by Ben Sayers as making it acceptable that club professionals should ask their members not to complain at waiting three months for the delivery of a set. We had no intention of gearing up to meet modern demand. What Ben Sayers considered important was that one man would complete the making of the set, virtually from beginning to end, and stamp the initial of his surname into the base of the clubhead, so that, should the club ever be returned as faulty, a deduction might be made from the wages as punishment.

18

In 1950 Ben Sayers himself, son of an illustrious golfing father, ran the factory with a rod of iron. He was not renowned for his generosity, a wooden-club maker received £8.00 per week and the iron-makers £6.00; as an apprentice I received thirty shillings. The factory was the tops as far as quality was concerned: not only were its clubs used by Royalty; even the Queen Mother's dolls' house sported a perfectly scaled-down set of our clubs, fitted into a tiny leather golf bag measuring about three inches.

The hand-forging I refer to was carried out in a dungeon-like forge at the furthest end of the factory, where a huge man, Jimmy Cluny, shook the streets of North Berwick with the vibrations from his great power hammer, as he shaped white-hot steel bars into clubheads with an accuracy that depended upon how many pints he had supped the night before, or what condition his digestive system was in. Once shaped, the heads were passed through to Jimmy Brunton, an expert at grinding and polishing iron heads, who later emigrated to South Africa and became a Club Professional in Durban. Following this, a set of nine heads would be given to an 'iron man', of which for part of my time there I was one, together with nine shafts, nine grips, nine cork underlays, nine ferrules, nine rivets, nine wooden plugs, nine plastic caps, nine each of red, white and blue disks, nine screws and a time-sheet to show how long it took you to turn the lot into a set of nine irons.

What took up most of the five hours to complete the task was the cork underlay for the grips. This, once the shafts had been successfully fitted into the heads and were cut to length, was wound around the top of the shaft so that it spiralled down about fifteen inches, and was sealed. Then, with the skilful application of a rasp, the cork was filed into a perfect taper, fairly thick at the top end but blending to the shaft at the other. The nine underlays were complete when the measurement of the diameter at any point matched identically that on all of the clubs; this was tested by means of a set of callipers. Then the wooden plugs were fitted into the top of the shaft and the leather grips wound on and rolled smooth.

It was at this point that old Ben would appear at the doorway and frown down on your workmanship.

'Are they accurate?'

'They're near enough, sir.'

'Near enough!' he would roar. 'Near enough's not good enough, they've got to be perfect!'

He would calliper down the set until he found some part a fraction thicker or thinner than the others, then slam them down.

'Get them right!' Off he would go grumbling and groaning.

19

Half an hour later he would return, by which time the grips had been refitted, tape had been added here, cork had been filed away there, and he would measure them again.

'They are perfect now, sir.'

He would not look up, but continue measuring, this time unable to find a single flaw.

'Aye, that's near enough.'

Many years later, when Professional at Dunham Forest Golf Club, I became the first British Club Professional to sign a contract with the massive Wilson Sporting Goods Company of America, as they made their inroads into Britain. I was taken to their factory, where I watched a very attractive young lady working a machine which fitted 1200 grips a day, each of them perfectly tapered and matched to the others.

Working in the factory as the very junior apprentice certainly provided quite a contrast to the Stock Exchange. There were tedious hours spent rubbing down the hickory shafts fitted to the most famous putter of the day, the Benny, its success due to the square look of the blade, which matched the squared-off top of the wooden shaft, all of which made lining-up easier.

Unfortunately there was, and still is, no better way of getting a hickory shaft to shape than by wrapping it in a sheet of sandpaper and working that up and down first using the one hand and then, as that arm became too weak, using the other. If by accident you continued rubbing just a fraction too long, the slimmer shaft became more flexible, in which case one of the tricks of the trade was to wind around the shaft a length of twine. This had the effect of stiffening the shaft, and it was a perfectly acceptable method, since the famous Bobby Jones' Calamity Jane had no fewer than three sections of twine. Indeed many requested this form of bracing in preference to leaving the shaft thick and therefore feelingless. Another trick of the trade, which I have used many times since, but which should not have been used in the manufacture, took place when the hickory shaft felt a touch insecure where it was inserted into the socket of the putter head. This was simply to immerse it overnight in a basin of water so that the wood swelled and the fit became tight.

The Benny putter possessed, like many of the Ben Sayers models, a grooved sole, the idea being to give the impression of the backswing movement 'skiing' along the grass, so keeping the motion smooth. This sole had to be polished on a special buffing machine to which an awful green soap was added. This was definitely a task for the factory's dogsbody, for though goggles were provided the rest of the operator's face became pitted with the green debris. I was responsible for this process until the next apprentice was signed on, some three months later, by which time, and much to the amusement of my fellow-passengers on the bus ride home, I was so impregnated I was turning green.

Another of the more tedious tasks that befell my lot was the turning of the blocks of persimmon. Endless hours were spent in the loft where old Ben had wisely invested in blocks of the precious American cherry tree from which the best clubheads in the world were, and indeed still are, made. Like good wine, these blocks were kept separate and were regularly turned to permit seasoning.

The method used was to place two slats of wood on the floor and bring the top row of these 'L'-shaped pieces of persimmon down, turning each over and placing it upon the slats. Once the first layer was established, another pair of slats was added and a second layer established, and so on.

Because of his wise investment in thousands of blocks, Ben Sayers was able to continue for years producing good woods whilst other makers suffered. Those who brought from America were purchasing unseasoned wood. The Americans were no fools: persimmon was in short supply, and they were certainly not going to give us the best – they kept that for themselves as they prepared to steal our show, which they eventually did.

As the unseasoned woods broke up, or swelled out of shape the moment they became damp, many manufacturers switched to untested forms of laminated wood heads and paid the price for having done no proper research. As junior apprentices we had not realized just how precious a commodity we were handling as we filled those boring hours in the factory loft.

3

•

THE SILVER CUP

It was around that time that a very wealthy American visited North Berwick and immediately fell in love with the town and the West Links, so much so that he decided to present a silver cup to be played for annually by the local golfers. He promised to present, in addition to the cup, another prize which the winner would keep, and he would return to North Berwick every year to perform the task.

This gesture pleased everyone, with the exception of old Ben once he found out the inaugural prize was a set of Gradidge woods and not a set of his own. Nevertheless the event took place and the winner was none other than Jimmy Brunton, that ace club grinder and polisher, who graciously received the silver cup and the woods.

What happened next I was able to tell, many years later at a dinner at the Circle Golf Club in Durban, which I visited as honorary Professional to the Eccentric Club, a famous London men's club which is, alas, no more.

It was on the Eccentric's tour of South Africa, when we were invited to play over that course, that I walked into the Professional's Shop and met, to my complete surprise, and after some twenty years none other than Jimmy Brunton; so naturally the tale of the silver cup was regaled that evening bringing great joy to the membership and a pink complexion to their Club Pro.

Jimmy was so proud of his Gradidge woods that he never stopped polishing them. Black tape was even added around the shafts so that there would be no chaffing by the golf bag. Unfortunately the silver cup did not receive the same treatment: after all, it was to be handed back the following year, so it lay in a cupboard in its box growing more tarnished by the day. This, of course, was no problem for Jimmy, whose skills as polisher would easily restore the cup to its original condition in time for the next playing.

One year later, on the Friday, the rich American was flying into Prestwick. That same day, being the eve of the competition, Jimmy turned up early for work, under his arm the huge box containing the solid silver trophy. Those of us who hadn't seen it gathered round as he removed it from the container and proceeded to cover it in the polishing soap.

It was a truly magnificent trophy, and we watched with eager anticipation, certain that Jimmy's skills would return it to its dazzling glory within minutes. Jimmy switched on his buffing machines and, as the motors warmed up, he took up his familiar stance and applied the silver cup to the first buff in the polishing process.

Whether it was the chill in the factory that made the soap tacky we'll never know; perhaps the machine hadn't warmed sufficiently. Whatever the cause, the silver cup was whipped from Jimmy's hands and disappeared in a flash up the duct which normally sucked in the ground metal.

Along the length of the factory ran a tube into which all the machine ducts emptied their debris. From there a great suction plant was used to draw all the waste and finally eject it into a bin at the far end of the building, by the forge.

Every member of staff stood frozen to the spot as North Berwick's silver cup rattled and crashed its way the length of the factory. Then, as one, we sprinted to the forge, where we found old Jimmy Cluny, who had been just about to place a waste bin in readiness for the day's production, standing in a heap of silver fragments, the largest piece no bigger than a sixpence.

The next day the silver cup was returned to the rich American in two golf-ball boxes. He left North Berwick and never returned, and Jimmy emigrated to South Africa.

4

CHRIS HANLON

My position with Ben Sayers was twofold. In the winter months I would spend my working day as a factory apprentice, then, when summer arrived, because of my wish eventually to become a Club Professional, I would move out to the shop Ben controlled or to the West Links, where I would act as an Assistant and give lessons to 'the rich Sassenachs' who spent their holidays in that lovely part of Scotland.

The only training I was ever given by Ben Sayers on the subject of teaching golf was to make the pupil tuck a handkerchief under his or her right armpit, and make them keep it there whilst they swung the club. Since, according to Ben, the Sassenachs all swung too upright anyway, this was all the cure I needed to know. Thinking back on this, the handkerchief really was an advantage: they could use it to wipe away the tears of anguish as they got worse instead of better.

At that time Ben Sayers also employed a young Irish Professional, nineteen-year old Chris Hanlon, who ran the shop all the year round. Those winter months were even longer for Chris than for me, for he worked away totally isolated in a shop which was unheated, except for one of those tiny Valor paraffin stoves.

The Professional's Shop which the tiny device was expected to heat, and where Chris would be found shivering, despite wearing his heavy black woollen overcoat, under which he managed to surround himself with three layers of pullovers as well as his waterproof overtrousers, was the site of the original Ben Sayers factory. Sunk into the ground to escape the gale-force winds, just below the first tee, the building comprised three sections. The frontage contained the showroom and, separated by a short corridor, the workshop, whilst in the rear of the building was the old factory, its ghostlike rows of workbenches standing unused since those skilled clubmakers of North Berwick had ceased to produce their superb clubs there and moved into the centre of the town.

Cold and unwelcoming though the shop was, to me, even in the worst of winter weather, just being allowed to visit it was a thrill, such was my desire to get out of the factory and into the environment of the professional golfer. So, when other apprentices hid or locked themselves in the toilets when they saw the huge golf bag being packed with ungripped, partly polished wood clubs, realizing that someone would be called upon to hump them the best part of a mile to where Chris would complete the task of fitting the grips, I would hover around the bag until ordered to make the delivery.

Just to escape from the noise of Jimmy Cluny's power hammer and the continuous whine of the grinding machines, and to be involved with a professional golfer, made the ordeal of struggling with the monstrous bag which contained the equivalent of some three sets of clubs, whilst leaning against the biting easterly wind that whistled in from the North Sea and stung your face with a mixture of sleet and beach sand, all worthwhile.

The round trip was just under two miles, but somehow I managed to stretch each visit to at least a couple of hours, during which time Chris and I could get outside on the grass by the first tee, swinging clubs and talking golf. It was necessary to come outside to get any feeling of being on a golf course, for old Ben had the workshop windows whitewashed to stop his staff being distracted from their duties by passing golfers, and this apart from having ensured that sufficient ungripped clubs were delivered to keep Chris from having the time to look out.

The young Irishman, who was soon to leave this his first professional's position and join King's Lynn Golf Club as their professional, where he is to this day, was a great one for playing pranks, often at my expense. His favourite, and one which I saw suffered by every new apprentice, was to unravel from a roll of pitched twine sufficient to complete the binding of the paper-thin neck of a wood, then, at the point where just a few more inches would be required to complete the task, the twine would be rested on the top of the vice and gently tapped with a hammer. The roll would then be rewound. The unsuspecting apprentice was challenged in a race to bind the neck of a club. Clubmakers pride themselves in the speed this can be done.

The technique used was to place the grip end of the club into the lid of a tin which was screwed to the upright of the workbench about hip high. The end of the twine, bent into an 'L'-shape and laid on the shaft just short of the club's neck, was then trapped there by means of a couple of spins of the shaft. You were then in the 'starting gate'.

The tensions built, the shaft rested on the left hip, the fingertips of the left hand lightly touching the top of the clubhead, whilst the right arm extended away from the club, taking with it some four feet of twine which was wound across the palm of the right hand. The pressure was taken up.

'Go!' The left hand would start to spin, increasing in speed until the fingers became a blur. The right hand pulled against the winding clubhead, reluctantly releasing only sufficient twine and so adding tension to the binding.

In my race with Chris, who of course had challenged me, he was at one bench and I at the other; the shafts gleamed and glinted in the light, as they spun with the speed of a drill. They were bending against our left hips, such was the pull on the twine. I was winning, I was going to beat the Pro! It was at that point that the piece of twine tapped by the hammer passed the point of no return, halfway between my pulling right hand and the bowing curve of the club's shaft. That is when it parts with a bang.

It's not the twine that bangs: the bang is the club hitting against the first object that gets in the way, usually the far wall of the building. You don't see this, for you have been spun violently in the opposite direction to the flying club. In fact nobody really sees what it hits, for they are usually all creased up in fits of laughter, having waited straight-faced for this moment. In this instance it was only my micky-taking Irishman, who had deliberately slowed up so that I might finish first; he was sitting on the floor convulsed with laughter.

I longed to get my own back, revenge is so sweet against a prankster. One very bleak winter's day the sky was absolutely laden with snow, and by mid-afternoon, when I made my delivery of gripless clubs, it was nearly dark. I had been instructed to send Chris back to the office whilst I remained in charge, and I decided to amuse myself. I was aware of Chris' hatred of spiders, which he would kill without hesitation, a habit which did not please the Scots, to whom the spider is a national emblem.

By climbing onto the bench and using the sharp edge of a chisel, I engaged my artistic talents to etch into the whitewashed window a spider's web. Soon the entire pane of glass was covered by a most convincing piece of artistry. Once I had added, right in the centre of the web, one of the biggest, hair-covered spiders ever, a species never previously seen in Scotland, the effect was quite dramatic, and the black sky above the old town of North Berwick against the whitewash made my spider absolutely lifelike. I was proud of my work. By the time Chris arrived back on the staff bike, the sky was even blacker outside and the spider even more lifelike. I met him at the door:

'Chris, I'm not going back in that workshop, there's the biggest spider I've ever seen!'

'Leave di little buggar to me.' Relishing the thought of another kill, he rushed through the passage way into the workshop.

'JEEsus, will you look at de size of that!'

I could hardly contain myself as he grabbed for it, but the funniest was yet to come. As his finger and thumb came together, with nothing between them, I expected the realization that he'd been had to take effect. Instead he rushed past me.

'Sure, di little buggar's outside!' Through the door he went, leaping over the fence in eager anticipation of catching the creature before it escaped. It was still there – Chris clutched at the hairy monster with such ferocity his fist went straight through the window.

We had quite a job explaining that to old Ben, but I had satisfaction.

5

———————————•———————————

ILL-GOTTEN GAINS

When spring arrived, just before the season was to begin, Ben would give the entire staff an early afternoon off to play in his works competition. The staff maintained that he did this to spot how many clubs had been stolen from the factory during the dark hours of winter. I didn't believe this comment until I arrived on the elevated 18th tee and looked toward the distant green. There was old Ben, perched on his seatstick by the back of the green. It became evident that he had some justification, as player after player completed the 17th hole then proceeded to attach and zip up the hoods of their golf bags, many of which contained one ancient club with which they played their second shot to the green, and an old putter to hole out.

Whatever the reasons – poor pay or just natural greed – items were removed using many ingenious methods, for golf clubs are not the easiest things to steal. One of the cleverest used was to take a set of irons into the upstairs toilet, together with a length of the golf club twine. A few minutes before the 5 p.m. bell was sounded, and long after dark, the toilet light would be switched out and the set of clubs, bound together by the twine, lowered to hang just above the ground in the poorly lit courtyard, whilst the other end was attached to a tap.

Once outside into the darkness, it was a simple matter for the thief to cut the string. Next morning when the factory opened, and it was still dark, the balance of the twine was pulled up and disposed of.

I hasten to add that I personally avoided such temptation for I know that I would have had such a guilty conscience I would never have hit a decent shot with such a set.

The management was aware of certain discrepancies and had long suspected one who came by bus from Edinburgh every day: after all, how could he afford the bus fare for the fifty-mile round trip on what they paid him, without another source of income? Those buses were always full, particularly during the summer months, and by the time the suspect and I reached North Berwick's terminal (for we travelled the journey together regularly) it was always standing room only. On the evening in question I had been kept late and missed my normal bus, but fortunately the next one came soon and was only half full. I took a seat whilst my companion, who had also missed our usual bus, remained standing in the aisle.

'Aren't you going to sit down?' I asked him.

'No, I prefer to stand!'

'But it's twenty-five miles to Edinburgh.'

'I don't care!'

At that moment the works manager and two large bobbies came onto the bus and asked him the same question. They already knew the answer. The set of woods, with their heads under his armpits and the shafts inserted down his trouser legs meant he couldn't sit down. He had counted on the bus being full but hadn't allowed for the extra time it had taken to walk to the bus stop with a set of clubs down his trousers, which had caused him to miss the busy one.

6

FIERY THE CADDIE

The long winter over, North Berwick and its superb West Links would come to life. The old caddies would come out of hibernation, having somehow survived the winter. Even in the summer when there was work about they still appeared as poor as church mice, living on a diet of pies and pints. How they had the strength to carry those huge bags, often 'doing a double' by carrying two bags for some of the American visitors, I'll never know.

The best of North Berwick's caddies was known as Fiery, no doubt named after the historic 'Auld Fiery'. He would arrive, wearing several overcoats, one upon the other, normally with the buttons in the wrong holes. Sympathetic visitors would give him gifts of clothes which he would put on top of those he wore already. It was questionable if he had ever seen a bathtub, and he stank something awful.

If we ever saw him approaching the shop, we would rush through the front door and meet him before he could get inside. Even then it was necessary to get upwind of him, for the smell was unbearable. Nevertheless stench, dirt, warts and all, everyone wanted Fiery as their caddie: for his uncanny knowledge of the greens upon which he had spent his life, across which he would peer through glazed methylated spirits eyes for some seconds before shuffling towards the hole, where he would point at a spot. That was the line, and heaven protect you if you didn't aim there – hence his name.

Once, when caddying for a good American player, Fiery stood by the bag on the tee of the famous Redan short hole, the 15th at North Berwick; the wind was behind and the golfer was throwing blades of grass in the air to test it. Fiery already had the no. 7 iron in his hand.

'Gimme the no. 8,' said the American.

'Ye'll tak the seeven,' replied Fiery.

More blades of grass went up and were whisked off towards the green.

'No! I want the no. 8.' Fiery handed him the club as if it was infected and walked off to the side of the tee, totally disinterested. The Yank hit a glorious shot; his friends were on their toes as the ball soared to the elevated green. One bounce, a few turns and it dropped into the hole. The four players jumped with joy, out came the whisky – back came Fiery.

'You'll take a wee nip Fiery,' said the elated golfer, a mischievous glint in his eye.

'Aye a' will that,' said Fiery. With the other younger caddies grinning at him, he knocked off half the flask in one go.

He handed it back, drew the back of his hand across his lips: 'It was still the wrang club!'

One of the early spring events in Scotland is the Ladies' Championship, and that year North Berwick was the venue. The favourite was a local lady from neighbouring Gullane (pronounced GULLane by the locals, GILLane by the English and GILLAIN in certain parts of Edinburgh).

Mrs Abercrombie was a huge specimen, built like a tank and always dressed, even on the hottest summer days, in a tweed golfing suit, thick wool ankle socks and heavy brogue golf shoes. On her head, a deerstalker hid the blue rinse. Her very presence put the fear of death into all the little ladies she came up against, above whom she would tower – hence her being the favourite for most of Lothian's titles, which she won with great regularity. When she approached the shop the assistants didn't rush to meet her; instead they hid in the back of the shop rather than face her. During the Championship Mrs Abercrombie's clubs were stored in the shop, where we cleaned them thoroughly after each round. Unfortunately, Mrs Abercrombie would not play North Berwick without Fiery, so after each day's victory she would stride in through the door with the ever-perspiring Fiery bringing up the rear humping the huge leather bag with its heavyweight clubs. It took hours for the smell to leave the shop.

Friday was semi-finals day and the pair, who normally finished off the opposition out in the country, were still engaged in battle when they reached the 18th hole. Both she and her opponent had driven down the centre, Mrs Abercrombie a good fifty yards further, of course. A huge gallery of tweed-clad ladies followed the match, standing silently, never daring to utter a sound or move a muscle when their heroine was playing, taking care of course to be upwind of the other half of the partnership.

In front of North Berwick's final green is a valley similar to the 'Valley of Sin' which lies across the final green at St Andrews, and the Scottish way of playing this is a running shot which descends into the valley then climbs the steep face. In those days unwatered greens on links courses were not receptive, so it was natural that Fiery reached into the bag for the trusty jigger, a short hickory-shafted club with the loft of a no. 4 iron, ideal for this running shot.

'Not that one, give me the wedge,' bellowed Mrs Abercrombie.

Fiery had refused to recognize this newfangled club which Gradidge and Bobby Locke had just launched on the market, and which would revolutionize the short game. He had seen it gleaming in the bag that morning but chose to ignore it.

'You're yin up wi yin tae play, she's miles awaw frae the pin. Ye'll use the chipper.'

'I'm using the wedge, it will give me a backspin.'

'Backspin?' roared Fiery, having never dealt with the subject in his entire life. 'Yer only fifty yards awaw, ye can putt it if ye want.'

The onlookers were stunned. Nobody had ever stood up to their giant of the links.

Not another word was said; Mrs Abercrombie pushed aside the trusty jigger and grabbed the gleaming secret weapon from the bag. Unlike the short stabbing swing that would have sent the ball scurrying across the crisp turf, had the jigger been used, instead the full flowing swing was engaged. It was unfortunate that instead of the heavy sole of the club biting into the turf just after impact, it caught the ball thinly.

There was a hush as the ball flew directly at the flag. Would it stop? All of Gradidge's advertising said it would. It didn't. One bounce by the pin and it took off; its second bounce was in the flower garden in front of the clubhouse; it was out of bounds.

Up the 19th they went; not a word was said between them, other than the mutterings between clenched blackened teeth as Fiery lugged the clubs into extra time up to the elevated green at Point Garry for the second time that day. Mrs Abercrombie, without the aid of her caddie, won the match there.

Back down the 1st hole the party made its way towards the Professional's Shop, the ladies surrounding their furious champion, urging her to forget the incident and on to greater things in tomorrow's final. The press had latched on to the upwind side of Fiery who, in typical caddie fashion and in earshot of his mistress, was describing the near-disaster in the way of all professional caddies:

'We hit braw drives a' day. We hit a' the greens an' we holed a' the putts, then *she* played that damn' newfangled wedge!'

Into the shop she stormed, ignoring us completely. Her entire wrath on this visit was to be spent on Fiery, who was still venting his feelings to all and sundry.

At last he arrived through the doorway where she stood, her clenched knuckles resting on her huge hips. 'I can forgive anyone for making mistakes,' she lied, 'but arguing on the fairway, then telling the press that *WE* played all the good shots but only *I* played the bad. That I cannot stand. I'm taking two shillings off your wages for that.' With that she stormed from the shop.

We felt that Fiery might not turn up for the final, but we were wrong. Through the door he came; we hadn't noticed his approach, for the wind had changed, even though he hadn't.

Mrs Abercrombie was already there inspecting her clubs in case we had missed a grain of dirt.

'Fiery, good you're early. I wanted to talk to you. I sat up in bed last night thinking over yesterday's events and I realize I was wrong and you were right. I should have run the shot up at the last, I made myself promise that I will take your advice.' She smiled benevolently: 'But just remember, we are a team and *WE* will keep it that way.'

By coincidence the final went to the 18th; both tee-shots were down the fairway; the opponent, much the shorter, had played a moderate shot to the edge of the green. The only difference was that the match was all square.

Without hesitation, for their ball was only feet away from yesterday's spot, Fiery took the trusty jigger from the bag and thrust it towards his player. Mrs Abercrombie didn't look at him; instead, staring hard at the green, she spoke:

'Give me the wedge.' The huge gallery shuddered. A stony silence fell over the arena. Tweed-covered knees trembled in anticipation.

'Ye'll tak the jigger 'n run it tae the pin.'

'I'll play the wedge. It'll stop today.'

With that she wrenched the dreaded glinting iron from the bag.

The swing was full. This time the impact was sweet. The ball pitched just one yard past the flag, then from the firm surface it leapt into the garden and out of bounds. The match was lost.

Writers and spectators stood in stunned silence, which was broken by Fiery, who at the full pitch of his rage roared: 'So much for a' they damn promises *WE* made in bed last night!'

7

VARIOUS VISITS
TO MUIRFIELD

Much has been voiced and no doubt written of Muirfield Secretaries, particularly, in recent years, of Captain Paddy Hanmer, who, to say the least could at times be difficult. Never more so than on the evening after Tom Watson's great victory in the Open Championship in 1980, when the new Champion and another famous American star walked back down the 18th fairway, from where they hit a couple of balls towards the green with an antique hickory iron which had just been given by a fan, and then returned to the dining-room of the Greywalls Hotel to enjoy a victory dinner with friends.

In stormed the Secretary and called the pair to him: 'The Championship finished at six o'clock. If you wish to play Muirfield, then apply to my office for permission!'

The American pair, courteous as ever, apologized profusely and returned, suitably chastised, to their friends.

A man with such power can be very forbidding and I recall being told of a meeting with him by a young pupil of mine who had been taken by his mother on a golfing holiday to Scotland. The lad, who was only fifteen years of age, yet had a 4 handicap, was carrying with him an introductory letter from me asking Club Secretaries that he be allowed to play their courses. It never occurred to me that they would go to Muirfield.

On their return, when they told me they had had their only problem with a Captain Hanmer, I shuddered, thinking this might be a racial problem, for although the lady in question is German, her husband is Indian and the boy has his father's colour and features.

'What did he say?' I asked tentatively.

The mother replied, for it was she who had informed the Captain that her son had a handicap of 4 and was a pupil of Alex Hay and could he play the course?

Captain Hanmer had ignored her completely, leaned across to the boy and said 'Take that woman out of the Clubhouse and come back, and I'll sign you in!'

My own first visit as an apprentice clubmaker, to the home of the Honourable Company of Edinburgh Golfers was not without incident.

Every morning and every night on my twenty-mile bus ride from and back to Musselburgh I would look seaward over the glorious links of Muirfield, wondering if I would ever play there, for neither young Assistant Professionals, nor apprentices were likely to gain the necessary invitation.

In fact I didn't play the course until I competed in the 1966 Open Championship; however, I did visit it – or, should I say, I visited as far as the Clubhouse door – when once a week, I used to cycle, on the staff bike, from the Sayers factory to the Clubhouse of the Honourable Company to check the stock of tees and balls.

Muirfield has never had a Professional attached, but it did permit Ben Sayers to display a set of his clubs in a rack and also place a box of Dunlop 65 balls, another of Dunlop Warwicks, and one full of tees behind the bar and in the care of the Clubmaster.

Checking the clubs was the domain of old Ben himself, and he was allowed into the Clubhouse to change them every now and again. Mine was a more humble task: in my saddlebag I carried spare balls and tees to replenish any sold over the weekend. I also had a tin box into which I would place any monies raised from such sales. My earliest experience of 'sale or return' business.

The first mistake I made on my very first visit was to park my bike against the wall by the front door. My second, and major, blunder was to walk through the front door, for it was there I encountered the Secretary.

'Out! Out! Out!' he screamed.

My two boxes of balls, my one box of tees and my float tin, from which I had removed the lid to show what an efficient service they would receive now that a Musselburgh man had taken over, flew into the air, scattering their contents in every direction. Balls, tees and money bounced and rolled all over that magnificently polished wood floor. I knew at that moment that my dream, indulged in as I cycled up the drive, that they might even invite me to play a few holes, was now well and truly dashed.

By then the Clubmaster, who was made of similar stuff to his master, had arrived on the scene, and I was removed, balls and all, to the front door. The ordeal was not yet over, for 'the bike' which I had carefully balanced by one handlebar against the wall, worried in case the brickwork might scrape the saddle, had lost its balance and rolled into a heap on the front step, and was now lying against the door. As my red-faced escort, a giant of a man, wrenched open the door in came the bike.

To say the least, I had no wish to visit Muirfield again, but I daren't tell old Ben what I had done, though he no doubt heard about it. Nevertheless, back I went the following week, this time careful to park 'the bike' against a high hedge well opposite the building: those who have ever owned a bike will know they don't fall over from hedges.

This time I walked to the door, having first secured all the box lids, and knocked, very quietly at first then gradually increasing the volume, until I was finally heard. The Secretary opened the door.

'You again,' he roared. 'Where the devil is that damned bike?' The scratches on the door were still evident.

'It's all right sir, I've parked it over there against the hedge,' I stammered, pointing to the ageing machine, glad to see it was still upright. His eyes became like organ stops. The veins stood out in his neck: 'That hedge! That hedge! That's the Captain's parking spot! Out! Out!'

Ben Sayers wondered what had happened to his trade with Muirfield members; his new delivery boy registered no sales for three consecutive visits. The first two I have described, the other I didn't make.

———————————●———————————

The next visit I made to Muirfield came during the 1966 Open Championship, the first won by Jack Nicklaus, the greatest golfer the world has seen. I had actually been involved in a play-off at nearby Luffness, being one of thirteen tied on 142 playing for one place. A very nervous seventeen-year-old had topped his drive, then his second which bounced between the guarding bunkers, and ran on to finish inches from the hole, so he was through. I had gone on fighting with the other twelve until, at the 5th hole, I eventually won the honour of first reserve for the Championship.

I carefully avoided using Muirfield's Clubhouse, changing by my car, in case I should be spotted. My practice rounds were beginning to convince me that I might just be in the wrong business. Championship

golf is the toughest test, all of the carries that year were over 200 yards, and the fairways (those I reached) were as little as seventeen yards wide and edged not with semi-rough but by foot-high grass. Later the Championship Committee took pity on the players and mowed a tractor's width on each side, making things even more difficult, for few could then find their balls and Doug Sanders asked for the concession on the hay. The course was then at the mercy of the longer hitters who could reach the distant fairways with iron clubs, as was proved by the mighty-hitting Jack Nicklaus winning and the Welsh giant, Dave Thomas, being runner-up. Shorter hitters committed to using drivers to reach distant fairways were simply not accurate enough to hit them all.

On the first day of the Championship I informed the starter where I would be found on the practice ground; I had spotted a quiet corner away from the main hitting area, where I could keep warming up gently in case I was called. In that way I would not interfere with the constant stream of competitors who had their scheduled starting times. I set off there with my caddie, a young Ashridge member, Howard Grigsby, the son of my dentist, who had asked to come with me to Scotland and experience the excitement of the greatest of championships.

I quietly went about my practice routine, starting with some short iron shots, working my way through the bag of clubs, Howard moving further out as I signalled him each time I changed up a club.

The standard signalling procedure from player to caddie became well exercised as the day wore on. Right arm extended means a slice to the right; left arm out a hook to the left; right hand only, waving towards the caddie, means move further away; and, finally, both arms waving together, away from the caddie, brings him in.

The day was broken by occasional visits to the starter. Were there any messages? Was anyone unwell? Anyone food-poisoned? Or just to remind him where I was practising, so there was no chance he wouldn't find me.

Howard had just emptied the bag of balls at my feet for the umpteenth time and was heading out once more. He was becoming quite expert at catching the balls just off one bounce, and there was no doubt I was becoming more accurate as the day wore on. I had never spent so much time loosening up in my entire life, but I was enjoying myself, the edge was there. Besides I had found a pleasant spot, being well out of the way and sheltered by large gorse bushes. I was not the only one to find this place, and a family had settled down for a picnic only a few yards away.

'Who is he?' I heard Mother ask.

'Never seen him before, but he must be good because they send the leaders out last,' said Father.

Howard was now catching regularly from one bounce. With my right arm I waved him away further, and started cracking 5 irons to him, again with monotonous accuracy.

'He's good,' said Mother.

'Very straight,' said Father.

'But is he long enough?' said brat.

'With my 1 iron, I'm long enough,' I informed brat.

My right arm signalled once more. Howard moved still further away. Because of the extra practice, I was now hitting 1-iron shots which were peppering Howard at around 200 yards.

It was then that I heard the stampeding feet, and noticed the dust cloud just beyond my gorse bush. Then he appeared, Jack Nicklaus himself, surrounded by hundreds who had seen him heading towards the quiet corner of the ground.

'Here will do, Jimmy,' said the Golden Bear, pointing to a spot not three feet behind my heels.

'Why there,' I thought? 'Surely he could go further away.'

Jimmy Dickinson tipped out the balls and headed off down the ground.

40

Brat called out to me,

'Go on, show him your 1-iron shot.'

Big Jack looked at me with those steely blue eyes, even the gallery hushed; no. 1 irons were not in common use in those days.

I had no option, I set up to the ball; I could feel those piercing blue eyes in my back, then I hit the sweetest shot, which bounced just in front of Howard, who caught the ball and tossed it in his bag. I was almost overcome with a feeling of relief.

Then I heard Big Jack call out to Jimmy who was now walking towards Howard, 'I'll open up with a few 7s.' I recall thinking how high-pitched his voice was and it occurred to me that he can't be all that strong, not with a voice like that.

I decided not to watch him; my confidence was now so high I thought I'd get another 1-iron shot in before he played, so I addressed the ball, the sun glinting on the knifelike blade of my no. 1 iron. I sensed all eyes were on me, not on him. It was at that moment that Big Jack's 7 iron impacted first with the ball then with the turf. The ground trembled; I swear I felt Muirfield move; my trousers flapped in the draught as the shaft cut through the air. The spectators gasped, then fell silent.

Two hundred yards away, Howard waited for my next shot. Suddenly I saw his head jerk backwards as Nicklaus' ball, still soaring, whistled overhead.

Howard turned back, his mouth agape. I put up both my arms and waved him in.

Now I was certain I was in the wrong business; besides, who wanted to play Muirfield anyway?

In 1980 I did return, this time as a member of the BBC Television Commentary Team to cover the Open.

The Director had called for additional rehearsal time: the Open is very important to directors, just as it is to us all, and we cover every hole, so we had spent a very hot morning watching all that our cameramen would show us the next day. At last a lunch break was called and Peter Alliss suggested we should all go to the Clubhouse for some food. I immediately suggested that perhaps a marquee would be quicker. This was ruled out, and we walked up the 18th hole from our position behind the 17th green towards the Clubhouse, towards Captain Hanmer.

The group approaching the Clubhouse included Peter, Harry Carpenter, Clive Clark, Henry Cotton, the Director, the Producer and me, all of us in sports shirts and slacks.

'Where shall we all meet up?' I asked.

'What are you on about, we are all here,' replied Peter.

'We can't go into Muirfield Clubhouse dressed like this, no Pro in his right mind would do that!'

'Don't be daft, you're with the BBC now and it's practice day!'

'I don't care, I'm going to change.'

They entered the Clubhouse and I waited for the secretarial roar; it never came. Nevertheless, I was not taking chances, instead I made for the car park and collected my bag. From there I made my way through to the locker room by the side door, gaining entry by showing my BBC TV badge, which was fastened to my sports shirt. I then changed into a pale blue pure cotton shirt, tied my navy tie, using a semi-Windsor knot, careful that the ends were dead level and that my Woburn Club crest, the symbol of the Duke of Bedford, was prominent. Next, into dark mohair slacks; then I slipped on my crocodile Foot-Joy casuals, and finally, my cashmere jacket, showing just the right amount of silk handkerchief. Finally I combed my hair, and I was ready.

I threw open the dining-room door and marched in. I was the only person in the entire room wearing a jacket! Captain Hanmer leapt from his chair: 'You've got no badge – get out!'

8

---•---

ANCIENT CLUBMAKING SKILLS
IN MODERN TIMES

As steel began to dominate the golf-shaft industry, hickory faded from favour, except in a few putters. Even in those, because it is vulnerable to warping, it began to lose favour, yet it is possible to straighten it – not by any engineering feat, steaming, or the like, but by rubbing it in the correct manner, a technique used by all the old clubmakers and which I have even used successfully to straighten steel ones which have been in argument with a tree.

In ancient times it was common for a putter shaft to be deliberately bowed forward from the top of the shaft down to the head. This gave a similar swing characteristic of the then illegal centre-shafted putter. Today the bowed shaft is illegal and all the curves and twists must take place within five inches from the sole of the putter.

Then each town of manufacture claimed the famous 'bend' as its own, with the result that ours was known as a 'North Berwick bend', and further north there was a 'St Andrews bend', and so on.

Causing the bend is a very skilful operation, and, if overdone, can weaken the shaft, especially if tried on a steel one. There is also the danger of burning or blistering the palm of the hand. Using the groove formed up the centre of the palm, a gentle rubbing up and down the shaft is applied. The pace must not be hurried, the pressure positive but not aggressive. It is continued until the palm realizes the shaft is becoming so hot it is about to burn, at which point the head of the club, which is resting on the ground, is turned in the correct direction and the two final rubs with additional pressure take the shaft where you want it to go.

It is inadvisable to chance three final rubs, unless you have an elastoplast handy. Should you push it too hard on that final adjustment, then that too is a mistake, for you will need a new shaft.

I was able to use this skill many years later at Ashridge Golf Club, playing with my dear friend Laurie Beasley, known to all as L.B., and a guest of his, Peter Meacock, a highly qualified engineer from Northampton. We had witnessed a display of putting over the first eight holes the likes of which neither L.B. nor I had ever seen before, or since. Peter was holing everything and seemed set to take our money.

On the 9th green, 'Cottons', named after its designer, Henry, yet another curling monster was holed, and all from an ancient hickory putter. Peter boasted of having found this club in a secondhand shop and had liked it from the first sighting. The only problem had been its twisted shaft, but being an engineer he had been certain he could straighten it, so he had purchased it.

First he had suspended it over a boiling kettle for a long period, then, when it was thoroughly moistened, took it down and applied pressure which straightened it. Fifteen minutes later it was bent again, exactly as he had found it.

Next was a more scientific method. The club was laid across two supports inside a tank, and weights of varying degrees, calculated by a computer, were attached at intervals along the length of the shaft. Then the whole lot was submerged in water for two days and nights.

Peter disconnected the weights, it was straight. Fifteen minutes later it was back where it started.

The process was applied again, but this time in boiling water. The same thing happened.

As he explained this, Peter handed the twisted antique to L.B. and me to examine.

'Just look at it, heaven knows how I hole putts with it. I'd give anything to straighten it.' He made his way to the 10th tee to take his honour, which he had enjoyed for most of the round.

As he teed up his ball, I took the putter from L.B. and started the North Berwick treatment, first rubbing the groove of my right palm up and down the shaft.

Peter was now taking a practice swing; I could feel the shaft heating up; he took up his address position by the ball, and looked down the fairway.

The shaft was becoming red-hot as his backswing started. I placed the toe of the putter into the turf. As I pushed forward the first time, his clubhead struck the ball; the second push down the shaft matched his follow-through.

44

As he turned, beaming, towards us, I said to L.B.: 'I can see nothing wrong with this shaft, can you?' L.B. took it from me and squinted along the shaft: 'Looks perfectly straight to me.'

'Don't be stupid,' said Peter. 'You must be blind, it's like a corkscrew.'

He took it from L.B.: 'Just look at it.'

He held it out before him, his mouth fell open. The old hickory was as straight as a gun barrel, and it has remained that way ever since. Peter never sank another putt all that day, and never has to this.

———————————●———————————

Another opportunity arose, more recently, to allow me to show off the long-lost skills. Leather grips, which were traditionally the best, fought off efforts to replace them by wind-on rubber varieties, until the advent of the slip-on moulded types of the fifties, when they were more or less banished, other than by odd discerning golfers such as Arnold Palmer who remained loyal to leather.

Winding a tape onto the shaft, soaking it with spirit so that it became sticky, and sliding a sleeve grip over the top reduced grip-fitting skills to the level of do-it-yourself club repairers.

Possibly because of the persistence of the great Arnold Palmer, the leather wind-on grip made a return to favour. It was common to see Arnie on the 1st tee unwinding an old leather grip and, with those powerful hands and fingers of his, skilfully putting on a fresh one, carefully fitting it edge to edge, so that you hardly see the join.

It was in the mobile workshop of the excellent Japanese club manufacturer, Mizuno (who provide a repair service to tournament players at all European Tour events), when they came to Woburn for the Dunhill British Masters, that I was able to exercise the benefits of my bygone apprenticeship.

Out of interest and curiosity I visited the large workshop which is staffed by a small army of Japanese craftsmen who complete all sorts of repairs and alterations at great speed and with great skill.

Because of my position at Woburn, I was permitted to stay and watch them work, and was delighted to see one winding on a set of leather grips, of the chamfered variety. These have the inside edges of the skins shaved very thin so that when pulled tight the spiralling leather comes neatly together.

The Japanese expert even had a roller, exactly as we used long ago: a heavy oblong block, with a wooden plug handle sticking up at one end. The shaft, with its newly fitted grip, was placed on a wooden board and rolled back and forth beneath the weight of the block and the downward pressure of his forearm. The result was a perfectly smooth tan leather grip. The club was taken from the assistant and handed to me for inspection by the beaming foreman, who bowed.

'Where did he learn to do that?' I pointed to the roller, primitive by their standards. 'Tokyo, 1985.' He was still beaming.

I took the club, and picked up from the dustbin a piece of packing string that had been discarded. Starting from the top of the club, I wound it, pulling on reserves of strength from long-neglected fingers, spiralling the string down the seams under which lay the dormant chamfered edges.

All the Japanese were watching in stony silence.

I then placed the club under the roller, gripped the handle and rolled it back and forward, up and down the string and leather. Then, as though I still did it every day, with my right hand, I tugged the string from the bottom upwards, the clubhead spinning in my left hand like a top.

There it was, the perfect chamfered leather grip, beautifully grooved down the seams. I handed it to the wide-eyed foreman: 'North Berwick, 1950!'

I left amid the 'Ah-so's!'

9

NATIONAL SERVICE

When I was called up to complete my National Service, having delayed it by joining Ben Sayers, I felt quite bitter about giving up valuable golfing time to spend two years in a uniform. I now look back on the time as one of the best periods in my life. Being trained as a typist at Hereford seemed so stupid, yet, with all of the writing I have become involved in, it has proved a tremendous asset to me.

More important, I learned how to duck and weave, a form of survival that I had never previously required, and to use any talents I had to get by. Perhaps that is why Peter Alliss always says of me that I have done the best I could considering my limitations.

Being a typist in the Orderly Room at an RAF Station put me in a privileged position where I could make many things happen, especially when there were many gullible young National Service officers in charge of things. One of the most popular practices, which made me many friends in the billet, was when I used to type myself a chitty which said: 'The undermentioned airman worked late last night, please provide supper.' Then I would add the Pilot Officer's name, for his signature, beneath which I would type my name, rank, and number.

Once he had signed it and left for his evening in the officers' mess, I would replace the paper in the machine and where I had typed the 'a' in airman very lightly, I would overtype an 'e' making it plural. Then under my name I would add a list of my friends, numbering as many as a dozen. The late-night mixed grill suppers were always the best meal of the day.

My Pilot Officer was full of praise for my willingness to work late almost every night, which in fact was only ever long enough to alter the note; and my accomplices were only too pleased to provide me with leave passes and additional railway warrants to enable me to get back to Scotland at every opportunity.

I recall relating this to the Air Commodore who was the Managing Director at Woburn when I arrived, and he, having been very much responsible for RAF training, did not look at all pleased – still less when I told him my favourite dodge, which was how to turn three days' leave into eleven; this one he didn't like at all.

The formula was to apply for the minimum allowance one was allowed to take at any time, that of three days. Being Scottish and being stationed more that 200 miles from home, I was then entitled to two days' travelling time. So Monday to Friday was covered.

Every weekend, unless on special duties, airmen were entitled to take a 36-hour pass from lunch time Saturday until duty commenced Monday morning. This was applied for the weekend following the official leave application and it was seen as perfectly reasonable to request of the Pilot Officer that, since I was going to Scotland until Friday night and already had a 36-hour pass from lunch Saturday, he would sign a chit to let me have Saturday morning off. Being aware of all the overtime I put in, he happily signed it.

Once a month every airman was entitled to a 48-hour pass from Friday lunch time until duty time Monday. So once a month I applied for this, making sure some time had elapsed since asking for my extended 36-hour pass. I then explained to another Pilot Officer that I was going on leave Friday lunch time; might I have a chitty to leave the camp first thing on Friday morning so that I might catch an early train? This being a reasonable request, he would sign the chitty.

After work on the Thursday evening I would present this chitty to the Sergeant at the guardroom, to whom I put it, having first told him that I was the one in the Orderly Room who processed all of his leave applications, that since the chitty showed me to be allowed off early on the next morning, might I be allowed to go now, so that I could catch the overnight train to Edinburgh. Even to him, a Sergeant in the RAF Police, it seemed like common sense.

So from Thursday evening till Monday week, eleven days was made out of three, and it could be done once a month; so this permitted me to play quite a bit of golf in Scotland. What's more, for the princely sum of adding another name to my supper list, it was possible to persuade local-living Welsh airmen to allow me to type an Edinburgh address on their leave form so they might claim a railway warrant; airmen were only allowed two a year, which was no good to them but ideal for my purposes.

48

It was because of one of those rail warrants that I did have one shaky moment. I had completed all of the processes, including adding a false name and number to the rail warrant, and since my train did not leave till nearly midnight, had taken myself to the cinema. Halfway through the main film a message flashed across the screen. It asked for an airman, giving his number, to report to the manager in the foyer. I thought nothing of this: Clark Gable, Ava Gardner and the African jungle were much too exciting for my attention to be aroused. Then it appeared again. Suddenly it dawned on me: this was my false name and number. I searched my pockets – nothing. I must have dropped my rail warrant when buying my cinema ticket. I was now sitting in a cold sweat, imagining the RAF Police waiting for me when they realized no such number existed.

I sat through the film without really seeing it, then at the close of the show I moved out with the audience into the foyer, maintaining a low profile. There were no White Caps waiting there.

I knocked on the Manager's door and explained that the name and number were mine, and could I have my warrant back. He informed me that he had telephoned the camp, but the person in charge of rail passes had gone-off duty, much to the surprise of the Pilot Officer who took the call: 'He normally works late at night.'

The Manager had posted the warrant to the address in Scotland which was written on it. 'At least you'll have a ticket to come back with,' he smiled.

Now I was in trouble: when the Post Office in Edinburgh realized there was no such place as Auchtermuchty Avenue, they would return it to its source, and the Orderly Room Officer at my station would trace it to its originator. All of these thoughts spoiled my leave, even more than having to pay for my fare home.

As I entered the camp gate eleven days later I expected to be arrested on the spot. A corporal who spotted me called out: 'Do me a favour, you work in the Orderly Room, would you mind handing in the mail?' He stuck a bundle in my hand. The top letter was in a buff-coloured envelope with the large black letters GPO printed on it, postmarked Edinburgh. I detoured past the latrines where, safely locked in, I tore open the envelope. Inside were the cinema manager's slit-open envelope, written across it 'address not known', and inside its contents, one rail warrant.

My good luck continued when I was posted for three weeks to the Rock of Gibraltar on an important RAF exercise, my task to type out the reports made by pilots who were searching for make-believe enemy submarines.

49

Unfortunately the typewriter I was to use had arrived two weeks before its operator and had been stood with the other equipment on the jetty, with the result that salt corrosion meant it was completely U/S. All of its keys were rigidly stuck and nothing would move them. This didn't matter too much since all of the aircraft's radar equipment must have stood on the same jetty, for none of it worked either; so there was nothing to record.

Because I was on duty all night, I was able to spend wonderful sunny days on the Rock or in the Mediterranean. At night when I reported for duty I was transported into the very core of the Rock, where one of those massive Operations Rooms you see on the Battle of Britain films had been carved out from solid rock.

The few who were on duty would curl up in chairs or on table-tops and try to sleep the night away. By the third night I decided to search along the row of doorways we had been told to stay out of in the hope of finding somewhere more comfortable.

Late at night all the main lights were turned down, we were at battle stations; there were just those bluish ones in the Ops Room. I opened the first door; in the darkened room there was someone snoring. I quietly closed the door, and tried another. Peering inside,

I could neither see nor hear a thing. I crept in, my arms outstretched feeling my way about, then I tripped over what felt like a rope and fell on the bed. Fortunately an empty bed, but an extremely comfortable one.

'This'll do me,' I thought. I pulled back the blankets and sheets and got in, boots and all, and slept like a log.

It must have been about 7 a.m. when all main tunnel lights were switched on; I didn't notice. I was sound asleep in the most comfortable bed the RAF had ever provided for me. My relief, having become concerned at my absence, had begun a search for me, as a last resort checking the private rooms, and it was he who woke me. It was then I discovered what had happened.

The rope I had tripped over was a thick white variety, draped between pillars surrounding the bed. I sat up, now able to study my surroundings only to find, screwed to the wall above my head, a large brass plaque on which was inscribed: 'General Eisenhower slept here, during the invasion of North Africa, 1944'.

We quickly remade the bed with the precision drilled into us during our squarebashing days, re-organized the pillars and left the room.

———————●———————

On the day I was demobbed I travelled to Musselburgh carrying a holdall containing my personal belongings and the kit-bag containing all my service gear. We were told to keep it for five years in case there was another war and we were called up.

I was humping the two bags from the bus stop at Eskside when I passed one of the town's dustcarts; its team had gone up an alley to collect the refuse. I had the sudden impulse to get rid of the lot, so I put my holdall down and grabbed the kit-bag at both ends and started to swing it. Just in time I stopped, untied the top and removed two items. Then I threw the bag and its contents into the gaping mouth of the truck: my military days were over at last.

I bent down and picked up the rest of my worldly goods, my holdall and my Air Force boots – after all there are not many boots that have slept in General Eisenhower's bed.

It would be wrong not to mention the kindness that was shown to me during my National Service by the members of various golf clubs, who were extremely helpful, allowing a clubmaking assistant the courtesy of their courses: particularly those of Alderly Edge in Cheshire and Fairhaven in Lancashire. They enabled me to keep a reasonable game going until I was able to follow my chosen career.

I recall sheltering from the rain beneath Fairhaven's Clubhouse balcony, waiting to complete a round. Waiting too were some elderly gentlemen, who were happy to pass the time of day with us. One made a profound statement that I thought little of at the time, but later learned to appreciate, and I think of him often.

'At nineteen,' he said. 'do you realize you could have as much as fifty marvellous golfing years ahead of you? Count your blessings, and enjoy them all. How I envy you, for mine have all gone, and yours are just beginning.'

How right he was. And I have counted my blessings, many times, with many a good cause.

10

---•---

BILL SHANKLAND,
'THE BOSS'

I was extremely lucky, on completion of my National Service in the Royal Air Force, to join the staff of one of the game's best teachers, Bill Shankland. I say lucky with all due respect to another excellent Professional by the name of Syd Scott. But for the strangest of circumstances, I should have gone to Carlisle City with him instead of to Potter's Bar with 'The Boss'.

Due for demob in 1954, I had written to Syd Scott in answer to his advertisement for an Assistant, taking great care to emphasize my clubmaking skills. Syd immediately replied, asking me to join him the day I was released; the job was mine. He took the letter and tossed it into the letter-box, and that is where it stayed, jammed in the metal casing of the box for over three months, in which time I had been offered a similar position with Bill Shankland at Potter's Bar Golf Club in Middlesex and had happily accepted it.

When the letter had released itself, a black mark on its corner where it had been stuck, it was forwarded to me. I telephoned Syd Scott, who had not understood why I had not turned up: Scottish Assistants never turned down such an opportunity. He had appointed John More, a contemporary of mine from Edinburgh, who couldn't believe his luck and who is still there as full professional. Such is fate.

Bill Shankland was, and still is, a remarkable man, whose story would have made one of the finest sports books ever written. An Australian, his father had come from Edinburgh; he was a natural athlete, who competed in many sports. He even swam for New South Wales against Johnny Weissmuller, hero of the Tarzan movies.

He came to England as a member of the Australian Rugby League team, with whom he gained some forty caps. He played for and captained Warrington, taking part in three cup finals at Wembley.

Rugby League over for him, he turned to his next love, golf, and soon turned professional. How close he came to winning the Open Championship, finishing 2nd and 3rd. What a pity his putting never matched his power and accuracy, otherwise he would certainly have taken the title.

He was, without doubt, one of the strongest and fittest athletes of his time; even now, well into his seventies, he is still a powerful man, as two young muggers were to find out near his home in Bournemouth. Both ended up in hospital: that is where he knocked them both, through the hospital fence. The police were going to charge him with assault until they found out how old he was; then they dropped the charges.

Most of his friends, who love him dearly, would claim that to get money out of him would have required more than two villains.

His great boast, that of being the hardest taskmaster any young Pro could work for, was borne out by many who left prematurely. Those who could stand the pace learned how to run a professional's shop and teach the game of golf.

The days there at Potter's Bar, where I joined him, were made up of teaching, being taught, cleaning stock and doing repairs. The discipline was exacting. Every penny had to be accounted for, even if we all had to stay on for hours locating a few pence when the till wouldn't balance.

Such a code would obviously suit some and not others. One that it did not suit, and who came after me, was Bill Shankland's greatest pupil, whose association ended in bitterness: Tony Jacklin.

Tony came from Scunthorpe as a talented teenager whose other option was to work in the steel mills of Lincolnshire. The Boss worked hard with him, and together they moulded a good method; to this day I can still see the Shankland grip when I look at Tony's hands. No lazy long thumb as seen in too many players today. Instead it is pulled well up into the hand, which encouraged good hand- and wrist-work.

Unfortunately, Tony became Shankland's worst Assistant, at the same time as becoming his greatest player. Time and progress have proved that you cannot be a good Club Professional and a successful tournament player at the same time; that is why the two factions finally split up over a decade ago.

Tony had no time for dusting stock, cleaning members' clubs, replacing spikes in sweaty shoes and the like. He wanted to play and practise. The Boss wanted lads who would do all of these menial tasks, thus providing a service to the members, so the arguments had to come and they did. The pair fought tooth and nail. The Boss had to keep him, for he was so good a player the members wanted him there. The fiercer the arguments, the more successful Tony became, until they could finally stand each other no longer and they parted company.

I was one who was good at polishing and cleaning, and I listened and learned so that I might become a good teacher; so I benefited from and enjoyed my days at Potter's Bar, tough though they were, particularly at the start – for the Boss would not make anything easy. He was always scrupulously fair, but if you wanted money you had to get out there and earn it. If you didn't you starved.

When I applied for the position advertised, the wage offered was £6.00 per week plus half of any of the fifteen-shilling lessons you gave.

I was offered an interview and on the very day I was demobbed I travelled from Edinburgh to Potter's Bar.

'You're just the lad I would have liked but I have just given the job to Reg Taylor, a very experienced professional. However, I could take you on at £5.00 per week and half of what you earn.'

'I'll take it.' So desperate was I to come south.

'Go home and talk it over with your parents and let me know.'

I couldn't persuade him to take my answer, so I returned to Scotland on the next train. I telephoned next morning and said I had talked it over and would like to come straight away.

'Good,' he replied, 'the job's yours, you start at £4.00 a week, plus half your fees.'

I remember thinking I had better get down there quickly or there would be no pay at all. So I arrived on his doorstep the next morning, having caught the overnight, Waverley to King's Cross, then the early morning mail train, back to Potter's Bar.

The Boss took me to some homes where lodgings were available. A very nice lady offered to take me in, full board, for £5.00 per week.

'That's a bit expensive for him, he's only getting £3.00 a week and half his fee.'

Another pound gone!

'I can only give him his bed and a boiled egg for that.'

'Fine,' said my benefactor. 'He can get some food at the Clubhouse.'

The food he referred to was the lunch prepared in a not very good kitchen and given to the caddymaster, who then screwed up his nose at it and offered it to his caddies. If none of them liked the look of it I got it, and I ate it. In my first six months there I lost over a stone in weight.

I remember going to the Boss's desk for my first pay packet; of course I had earned no fees during my first week, so was terrified that there might be any further drop in my pay.

'What was it we agreed? £3.00 I believe.'

My heart lifted, I could pay my lodgings.

'Less National Health stamp of 6s. 9d., that leaves £2. 13s 3d.'

Realizing I might be in some financial difficulty, the Boss offered a solution: 'Why don't you come in on your day off and Simonize my car for the price of a lesson?'

I agreed, I needed the money. Waxing a Daimler was a hard day's work, but finally it was done and I went for my money.

'There you are, one lesson is 15s. and I get half.' I was handed the 7s. 6d. I paid my lodgings and had 9d. left. And they say it's hard for young Professionals today. If only they knew.

I would never wish anyone to think that Bill Shankland was mean: he was not, and he was scrupulously fair, but he was a man who had lived hard and had driven himself to the top in everything he had done. He had an intense pride in everything he had achieved. As a young Rugby League player, he would train harder than anyone else, often taking himself off to quarries and voluntarily shovel and swing picks just to toughen himself up. Those demands he put on himself were the principles for the high standards we had to set for ourselves if we were to be called Shankland Assistants.

'I don't care what a man does for a living,' he would roar at us; 'if I had to shovel shit for a living then I'd be the best shit shoveller in the world!'

Another point he would hammer into us, when he was criticizing the appalling record of golf teaching was 'Golf needs clarification.' This because so many contemporaries would give a lesson by saying 'Watch me' then proceed to swing as they were naturally gifted to do, expecting the poor pupil to observe and copy. We learned to diagnose and analyse, within three shots of meeting a pupil, then explain properly how best improvement could be achieved.

56

It was tough learning, but it was worth learning, and anything worthwhile must be paid for. I paid my dues!

Bill Shankland was so gentle and charming with the ladies, they all adored him, broken nose and all, but his aggressive attitude surfaced on the teaching ground or during arguments, some less friendly than others.

Soon after I joined him, we all played in the Middlesex Open, won that year by Arnold Stickley, the popular professional from Ealing, who was a stylist rather than a hitter, but unfortunately after a few celebratory drinks in the Ealing Clubhouse, in those far off days when professionals hung around after collecting their prizemoney, he announced to the gathering how strong his hands were becoming.

'Strong!' bellowed the Boss. 'Strong! You don't know what strength is!'

'You don't need to have chain marks around your ankles to be strong!' retorted the angry Arnold, backed up by the other Club Professionals in the group, reminding the Boss of his Australian heritage.

This was too much for the Boss who, turning to the barmaid, asked for a beer-bottle top. He handed the serrated edged cap to Arnold:

'Put that between two fingers and bend it.'

'Go on, Arnold,' the others urged and Arnold did, fitting it between his forefinger and middle finger, squeezing away until blood began to appear between the metal edges.

'Impossible!' he banged it down on the bar top.

The Boss's face was a picture: 'Give me three more, my dear,' remembering to turn on his charm to the barmaid, who watched, as we all did, in fascination. The three, plus Arnold's bloodstained but still perfectly shaped top, were carefully fitted between the five fingers of the biggest, strongest hands I've ever seen and slowly, and without as much as a change of expression from the owner, rendered into perfectly flat half-moons, at which point, by turning his hand over, the Boss laid them out gently on the bar-top, where they rocked gently.

———————•———————

Potter's Bar is one of the country's Jewish Golf Clubs, by which I mean that the membership is predominantly Jewish, for, despite a large number of 'Christian' clubs who bar Jewish members, no such case operates in reverse. However, they are normally expensive to join, giving a high standard of service and providing for the members the best of staff, and for the staff the best of equipment.

In those ten or so clubs scattered around the country the predominant trades and businesses of the area are well represented; for example, Manchester's Jewish clubs have many in the rainwear trade. Potter's Bar had a lot of its members in ladies' clothing (the rag trade), so many of Shankland's pupils were more used to handling delicate fabrics than wielding golf clubs.

One such pupil was Johnny Parnes, who used to annoy the Boss, for Johnny was potentially a very good golfer. However, because of weak hands, his hold on the club used to deteriorate from the perfectly formed right-hand finger grip of the orthodox Vardon design, which was normally a feature of all Shankland's best pupils, and which the Boss had taught him over long teaching sessions, and would revert to an ugly palm grip – something most learners do in early efforts at the game.

The result for Johnny was invariably a smothered hook which disappeared into the muddy ditch which separated the teaching area from the course, and which certainly meant another ball that would never see the light of day. Old Shankland could only stand parting with so many of his practice balls, and finally, after carefully positioning our Johnny's hands on to the club and explaining, for the thousandth time, having just been asked again for the thousandth time 'What caused that?' the Boss stood back, teeth clenched, to allow the hit.

At the very instant the backswing was about to commence, Johnny's fingers released from the position sculptured so painstakingly by one of the world's best teachers, and were about to revert to this ugly fisty grip, which his subconscious preferred, when the Boss struck. This was the 'once too often that takes the self controlled beyond their brink'.

Like the best of Australia's wing three-quarters, Shankland dived forward, arms outstretched and caught Johhny's hands before the clubhead had travelled a couple of inches. As he grabbed, the Boss, in one violent movement, remoulded the fingers, and squeezed them with such determination. Johnny would never forget again.

From the Professional's Shop, some sixty yards away, we all heard the scream and dashed to the doorway. Members who were practising on the putting green stood frozen to the spot. Johnny was now being helped across the bridge, his fingers crushed and moulded into the perfect Vardon grip, a position in which they remained, he claimed, for several weeks to come.

When he did come back, his golf did improve, though his name never went into the appointments diary again.

Johnny Parnes was one of a great bunch of members who worked hard all week, enjoyed their weekends at the Club and had a great sense of humour, so exaggerated renditions of the occurrence provided great fun all round, especially when the Boss claimed he 'hardly laid a finger on him'!

In every golf club, there are some difficult members who, with only a little effort can become intolerable. We had one, whose name I shan't mention, who had left a golf bag for repair. Stitching the bottom of leather bags was something we couldn't do, so it had to be sent off to the Spalding factory at Putney. Several weeks had gone by, during which our client had accused us of not sending it off, not caring, hoping he would buy a new one, and other reasons for its non-return.

Eventually, after several telephone calls, it arrived, along with an invoice for £2.00. To our surprise, the Boss decided that the owner had waited so long he would charge no profit margin, simply cost plus the postage incurred of 10s. each way, a total of £3.00.

The Boss was working away at his desk in the corner of the showroom when in came our customer.

'I've telephoned Spalding and they posted the bag weeks ago.' Typical of company policy to pass the blame to the retailer. 'What's more, they told me the cost!' No company should ever do this.

We couldn't wait to hand him the bag, in the hope that he would leave the premises, for the Boss hadn't looked up. A bad sign.

'You only have to pay a pound for the postage on top, that's a total of £3.00,' I said, imagining how pleased he would be, knowing how this man used to throw his money about like a man with no arms.

'£2.00 they told me, and £2.00 is all you'll get,' was the reply, and two pound notes were flung down on the counter.

The Boss was rising from his chair, not like the Australian wing three-quarter, more like a caged animal about to spring.

'We had to pay 10s. postage to send it,' I insisted, 'and there will be 10s. charged for its return.'

'That's all you deserve, you thieving lot, and that's all I'm paying,' our customer announced bravely but foolishly, reaching for his bag and turning for the door. He never reached the bag, but the door he certainly did. One of those massive hands had him by the back of his collar, the other had caught him by the seat of the pants, engulfing considerable flesh as it did, and our customer left screaming, across the threshold, feet clear of the carpet, from where he was launched head over heels across the putting green, rolling along like a curled-up hedgehog. His golf bag followed and, much to our surprise, the two pound notes.

To its credit, the Golf Club Committee, once it had heard the truth, insisted that the Boss be sent an apology, which he was.

11

———————•———————

JOHNNY RISCOE, DOG-LOVER

Somehow in those days there was a very good spirit between the members of clubs and their Professionals and Assistants. Not that I am complaining about today's members, for I think that in those days, even at the humblest of clubs when fewer played the game, members were the businessmen and professional people who recognized that young Assistants were only one week's wages away from the poverty line. Today you can understand the different attitude of some who see playing Professionals being paid vast sums, shops full of expensive stock, and young Assistants driving around in their costly cars, covered in sponsors' clothing, much of which, I hasten to add, they work long and hard to earn. Nevertheless, the gap closes and members feel it unnecessary to provide financial aid.

In those days any Assistant being taken out would be paid to play. If taken to another club, his expenses would also be covered. Whilst I am sure there are still many who provide such generosity, there are those who feel that youngsters being paid to play is unnecessary. They even play against the lads for money, using their club handicaps and insisting the front tees are used. I wonder sometimes, if you asked one of these gentlemen to spend four hours of his working day with a client and then charge no fee, how he would feel about it, when such hours probably bring him in twenty times what the young Professional would charge anyhow.

Members of Potter's Bar used their Assistants well, and once a few clients were acquired lodgings could be paid 'up front' and treats, like regular meals, could be expected. However, before such business could be relied upon we used to look forward to a Friday, when that humorous little man, Johnny Riscoe, a well known theatrical agent who today does great work with his daughter, Patsy, for the Variety Club Charity, used to turn up at lunch-time with a great paper bag full of what we called 'Jewish Fish'. Cold white fish, with all sorts of pickles, and absolutely delicious. We would settle down in the workshop and devour this meal and listen to Johnny's jokes and the Boss's great stories and laugh well into the afternoon.

Johnny Riscoe and his good friend, Willie Fox, a lawyer, who was blessed too with an extraordinary sense of humour but who, like Johnnie, was no more than five foot six inches tall, invited my fellow-Assistant Jeffrey Coleman, now Professional at Pontefract Golf Club, and myself to a day out at Wentworth. They would pick us up by car and treat us to the entire day. I could hardly believe that I was going to play the famous Burma Road, where Mr Aitken had been a Professional.

Eighteen holes in the morning over the great West Course, a huge lunch, then out we went on the more gentle East Course, by which time it was late into the afternoon.

The two Assistants were playing against the amateurs; after all there was no point in Jeff and I taking each other's money. We had won the morning game and were doing well by the turn on the East. Riscoe and Fox were fiercely competitive, especially Riscoe, and not keen to lose twice in one day.

It was very hot when we reached the short 10th hole, set in the trees and bordered by the sort of houses I'd never seen before other than on films. Possibly it was the heat which had affected an extremely large St Bernard, which lay panting on the grass by the driveway to its home, just by the tee. Whatever, it had turned the great creature into what could only be described as 'fruity', with the result it wallowed over to the tee and started sniffing around, none of us keen to argue with it, since Jeffrey, at five feet eight inches was the tallest member of our group, whilst the beast must have measured eight feet end to end – matched, I must add, in equal proportion by its reproductive parts.

This great monster followed us to the green, which, surprisingly, under the circumstances, we had all hit with our tee shots, and stood watching us putt out. Jeff, Willie and I had hurriedly putted and missed, leaving Johnny, who was closest to the flag with a tricky twenty-footer, downhill and with quite a curve. Never the fastest of players, he carefully lined up – a 2 was imprinted on his mind.

Up to the ball he crept, his eyes only leaving it momentarily, when his gaze fixed on the hole. This was to be the precision putt of the day; this would be the turning-point. Finally he was settled, crouching well over the ball in his familiar pose, knees bent and knocking, elbows splayed to allow the freedom for the smooth pendulum-like putting stroke. It was then that the dog mounted him.

62

At full stretch this canine resembled a great hearthrug, its massive paws flung around Johnny's shoulders, the slobbering tongue licking at his ears, the heavy moist, panting breaths steaming up the wee man's glasses, whilst its masculinity gleamed in the sunlight.

By now the rest of us were either convulsing with laughter or sitting down in case 'fang' should change its mind and select another mate.

'Help me, help me for God's sake!' pleaded Johnny, still over his ball, the putter head suspended in mid-stroke, a couple of hundred-weights of St Bernard engulfing his tiny crouching frame. With his right shoe he was trying to fend off the offending weapon. 'Help me, Willie!' he pleaded. Willie walked up as near as he dared, had a good look and said in his calmest voice, 'It comes in from two feet on the right, and don't be short!'

Johnny and I laugh about that dog every time we meet, and I remember, years later, telling a group of fellow-professionals of the incident. We were practising for the DAKS tournament and we stood on the same tee. I pointed out to them the house from where the dog had come. This was the first time I had noticed the name carved on the gate, 'The Mountings'.

———————————●———————————

Probably because of Johnny Riscoe, Bill Shankland had a marvellous relationship with the Vandeville Golfing Society, a group of which today I enjoy the privilege of being among the Honorary Professional Members.

Between them they used to organize a wonderful day at neighbouring Brookman's Park Golf Club, where the Boss had a lovely home and where he, his charming wife Daphne, and his sons Bill, Craig and Dale were all members. He had met Daphne on his first trip with the Australian Team; she, a New Zealander was a pianist on the liner.

The VGS members would be entertained by Club members to lunch and golf and then would stay on and give a concert party in the evening. Artists such as Charlie Chester, Al Read, Donald Peers, Ted Ray and the like were all guests, and my wife Ann and I, recently married, were always invited.

They were great days, enjoyed by all until one day they made the mistake of inviting the Singing Cowboy, Cal McCord, whose contribution after the golf was to get into his cowboy suit and ride his horse into the clubhouse, which he did singing at the top of his voice, cheered on by members and staff, until the horse crapped in the centre of the new dining-room carpet, whereupon the Steward resigned.

Bill Shankland had many Assistants, some who stayed a long time and others whose residence could be timed in minutes rather than days. Such individuals never have a kind word to say of him, and I daren't repeat what he says of them. But those who did last the pace learned their trade, and most have gone on and done pretty well for themselves; all have a deep and lasting affection for the big man.

When I left after four years' apprenticeship, I was replaced by Colin Christison, who is now the Club Director of El Paraiso on the Costa del Sol. It was as Junior Assistant to Colin that young Tony Jacklin was assigned in his first professional appointment, and he came from Lincolnshire as a very confident young man.

After work he would challenge Colin and the other Assistants, who were no mugs either, to play for ten shillings, then would find by the end of the week that much of his wages had been lost. Fortunately Tony had a reasonable singing voice, so he introduced himself to the Manager of the Railway Inn at Potter's Bar as an expert on Elvis Presley impersonation, which he then did most Saturday nights and so funded himself through those early days until he stopped losing money and started winning it – a habit which, once acquired, he continued, right through to those marvellous victories of the Open Championship in 1969 and the United States Open in 1970.

Through those early days the Boss spent more time with Tony than he ever did with the rest, for Tony wanted so much to learn about his own game, being totally uninterested in that of others. Fair comment, for that is the stuff the best tournament players are made of. However, that is not what Shankland, brought up in the era where you were a tournament player Wednesday to Friday then, after a mad rush home, a Club Pro looking after your members Saturday and Sunday, wanted of an Assistant. So arguments took place until an awful friction had built up, saved only when the members of the Club decided to retain Tony as a tournament Professional totally separate from the Shop; and so the two powerful personalities were parted.

This was unfortunate, for they both owed each other a great deal. Tony must be ever grateful for the many Shanklandisms I see in his swing. His beautiful grip, the perfect set-up of his posture, the emphasis of width at the base of the arc as the clubhead approaches low towards the ball; all Shankland assistants were roared at: 'Width means power!' To him long, looping swings meant nothing. He was

64

often accused of having a shorter backswing than all other professionals. 'Maybe so, but it's a damned sight wider than all of theirs!' So too was Jacklin's.

On the other side, whilst Bill Shankland should have realized that the Jeff Colemans, Alex Hays and Colin Christisons were potential Golf Professionals, men who could generate a living from giving a service over all aspects of the sport, he should have seen that in Jacklin he had his first real professional golfer, one who could make it to the very top purely by his playing talent. The Boss didn't realize there was room for such an individual and so failed to cash in on this prodigy.

What a pity the immovable object met with irresistible force, when each had so much to offer the other.

12

────────●────────

MY OWN JOB –
EAST HERTS

Once an Assistant Professional has completed his training, he sets off to gain his first job; this is the hardest to get, and it usually means applying to a smaller club, even a 9-hole course, from where a capable young man will work his way up a ladder of clubs, hoping that one day he might achieve a Wentworth or a Sunningdale or a Gleneagles or even a Woburn.

My own ladder started with East Herts Golf Club, then on to a new Jewish Club, Dunham Forest in Cheshire. The call of the south brought me back to the lovely Ashridge Golf Club, where I hoped to stay forever; that was, until I was invited to play at Woburn, and that next rung just had to be climbed.

To say that the original East Herts – for the present East Herts exists in much more luxurious surroundings near Buntingford – was a very friendly little club would be an understatement. Its social activities had gained it another name, that of the Easy Tarts Golf Club, but that is all I will say on that subject.

Set high on a chalk ridge high above the Ware Valley, it was one of the driest courses for miles around, so attracting many visitors when the muddy courses of Hertfordshire and Middlesex closed down, deep in mud.

The whole course had been owned by a very wealthy miller, who at a very good age had recently decided to give up the game and sell the entire place, clubhouse and all, to his fellow members for the grand sum of £4,000.

The Members' Committee met to discuss this offer and duly arrived, in its wisdom, at the decision that the offer should be turned down, since, they were all agreed, Mr Ward, who

66

was exceedingly rich, would give them the course for nothing.

Mr Ward did nothing of the sort; he simply added a few hundred pounds more and sold it to McMullens, a local brewery, who acquired what must have been the best purchase of their entire lives, for only a few years later a major road was built through the centre of the course and sufficient millions in compensation were paid – so much so they were able to buy a new East Herts and give it to the members. They then sold the half of the course which lay on the wrong side of the new road for development, reaping in still more millions, and after all that they still have the Clubhouse and the best 9 holes, which they run as Chadwell Springs.

The other 'wise' decision that particular Committee made was to engage me as its Professional.

I was not the first Professional that the Club had, for there had been several before me, but I was the first full Professional. The others had been Greenkeeper Professionals, and indeed my poor predecessor had given up because they had worked him into the ground. His duties had been as Greenkeeper from 7 a.m. until lunch, where he helped his wife cater. From 2 p.m. he became the Professional, teaching and selling. Then at 6 p.m. he became the Steward and ran the bar until those last, lingering members departed sometime after midnight. It was after Bill's parting shot that the Committee decided to get one of each: a Greenkeeper, a Golf Professional and a Steward.

That parting shot was delivered in a fairly original manner from a most unusual position. Old Bill, having overheard murmurs of criticism for, would you believe, not working hard enough, decided to perch himself on the rafters of the roof above the Committee Room so that he might hear what was in store for him.

Crouching there in the darkness, hardly daring to breathe, he listened to his fate being discussed. Unfortunately, the cold got into his limbs and he took cramp. His efforts to gain a new position had almost been successfully completed, though Committee members swear they thought they had heard something when Bill misjudged his footing. He crashed through the ceiling, one leg coming through the plaster either side of a large beam which, though it saved the Greenkeeping Professional Steward from serious injury, provided sufficient of a lesser variety to render him momentarily silent.

This silence was matched, once the plaster and rubble had finished hitting the Committee table, by the entire group, who looked up at a pair of hairy legs, their owner still unrecognizable, until finally the balance of the ceiling gave way, to expose the bulging-eyed Bill.

It was at that point that the luckless Bill made them aware of what they could do with their job. This was duly recorded in the minute book.

The first of the newly available positions was filled by a Greenkeeper who had been a prisoner of war but had been trained in greenkeeping before the War, on the links of Westward Ho! He had moved to Hertfordshire with his children and was found working in a filling station.

He was Scottish, and obviously an intelligent man, who found several flaws in the way the course had been maintained, one of these being that the elderly Assistant Greenkeeper, 'old George', had mown the greens using one of those awful overgreen machines, in the same direction three times every week for about ten years.

The direction and the order in which they were cut was important to George, for they had to fit in with the opening hours of the pub below the course in Ware Road to which he had worn a footpath.

The continual cutting in one direction only, and using those terrible machines produced a grained grass, for in those days there were no verticutters, with the result that it was possible to pick up the end of a blade of grass and unravel it like a knitted jersey until you had in your hand a blade of grass six or seven feet in length. The incoming Head Greenkeeper's decision to redirect the cutting met with fierce opposition from both George and the local publican, both of whom had the ear of the Club Committee.

Known for its wisdom, this Committee decided that the new man didn't know what he was talking about and so appointed the Chairman of the Green's Committee to draw up a programme for him to follow. Three times a week the Chairman would drive up to the Club to ensure that his directions were being followed.

It was fairly obvious that a chemist, then the following year a haulage contractor, were not likely to know a lot about greens, neither having done a day's gardening in their lives; nevertheless, it had been decided that they would advise our man, who fortunately possessed infinite patience, probably gained in the prison camp, and who accepted with a silence which seemed strange to me, for he appeared to know a bit about the subject. So much so that he was offered the post of Head Greenkeeper with that superb Scottish links at Longniddrie, a position he kept only for a couple of seasons, whereupon he was snapped up and became the Links Supervisor in charge of all the courses of St Andrews.

There were those on the East Herts Members' Committee who considered they taught John Campbell everything he knew. They duly congratulated themselves and recorded as much in the minutes.

I should not be too critical of those gentlemen of that Committee; after all, they did give me that all-important first position, but then perhaps it was because they had a lady golfer on the interviewing panel – a fairly unusual step, and one that, being Scottish, I must admit frightened me a bit, for in those days women did not have too much to say in golf where I came from. There is the old saying that 'women should only be allowed to play after four o'clock', to which is added 'in the winter'.

This lady was the Ladies' Captain, and so determined was she that her team should do well in the Pierson Trophy, a very special club event for ladies in the North London area, that she insisted on having a say in who should be the next team coach. She got her wish; after all, she was bigger than any of the men on the Committee, who were all terrified of her.

There can be no doubt that she secured the position for me. Her questions on teaching and repairing clubs were all perfect for me, and my pedigree with Sayers and Shankland was just what she wanted.

Once I had the job I thanked her profusely.

'You're just what I want for my team.' Then, wagging a finger at me she warned, 'Just don't do what your predecessors have done, and you'll be fine.'

'What was it they did?' I asked foolishly.

'Never you mind, Hay. Just get on and teach my team!' The formalities were over. I dropped the subject, but I did get on and I started filling my diary full of enthusiastic ladies, all encouraged by the Lady Captain and hoping to be transformed into members of her Pierson Trophy team.

At last my first teaching day as a full Professional arrived. My wife Ann came to the club to look after the little wooden hut, into which we had ploughed our entire savings in golf merchandise, and I headed off up that galeswept hillside to the top, where the practice ground lay, to join my first pupil and prospective team member, Mrs Noble.

Fortunately at the end of the practice ground on top of that exposed plateau grew a massive gorse bush, in the lee of which teachers at East Herts could safely tuck themselves, together with their pupils, and escape most of the gale.

Once Mrs Noble and I had established a fairly sheltered position, I emptied out the bag of practice balls and suggested she have a few swings to loosen up before her first efforts at hitting the ball. I made the observation that she must be feeling a little nervous since her swing looked, to say the least, a bit rigid. 'Oh, I am, Mr Hay. I'm so keen to make the team, and the Ladies' Captain says we've to do exactly what you tell us.'

A few more exercise swings, none of which inspired me with any great confidence, and I suggested we try a ball, which I deliberately teed up fairly high.

Mrs Noble had obviously been told that a good body-turn would add distance; however, what she must have misunderstood was that this should be accomplished by the swing, not by turning her feet so that her back was almost facing the hole as she addressed the ball.

From this impossible stance the inevitable happened. The backswing was a pick up of the club, which, without any body resistance, continued until it passed horizontal and dangled towards the ground. From there, it wasn't so much a downswing, as an attempted recovery, the clubhead running out of power as it neared the ball. The result was a shot that floated through the air and landed gently some forty yards from where we stood.

Tact is one of the essential requirements of the teaching professional. Patience another.

'Now then, Mrs Noble, you need to loosen up a bit, try another.' I teed up another ball.

The routine was identical, the ball, fluttering rather than flying, landing right by the previous effort. Was this how I was to spend the rest of my career, watching swings like this?

'Mrs Noble,' I said quietly, not wishing to make her nervous, 'is this how you hit the ball?'

'Oh no,' came the reply. 'You've inspired me. I've never hit it this well before.'

I was now determined that my first lady pupil would succeed. Taking her club and standing her to the side, I prepared to demonstrate what she must do.

'By closing your body out by the way you stand, you cause an overswing when going back, then you are unable to gain a follow-through when you return, so the impact jars the ball instead of striking it through.'

I suggested she tried picturing the swings of Dai Rees or Bernard Hunt, who were the local Hertfordshire heroes, there being no Seve's around in those days.

70

'Watch this.' I stood with an open stance, so that my right foot was forward and my left hip towards the flag, then I swung a practice swing.

'Note how the backswing is short.' Then I made the full follow-through I wanted for her and held the pose. 'Look how my hands are high and the club has wound fully around my shoulders. See how my weight is right through onto my left foot and my right shoe only has the toe on the ground.'

I could see she was suitably impressed and couldn't wait to get back into position to try it, especially when I guaranteed at least three times the distance she was getting.

Mrs Noble made six or seven dummy runs and I have to admit was beginning to look very good. At last, I decided, it was now or never.

'Mrs Noble, I'm going to tee up the ball, but I don't want you to worry even if you miss it. All I want is 100 per cent effort to the follow-through. Do you promise?'

'Oh I do, I do!' she proclaimed. 'I'm so determined to make the team. I won't let you down.'

Mrs Noble didn't let me down; in fact she hurtled through the ball like a hot knife through butter, on her way to the fullest throughswing of her life.

The ball rocketed from the clubface untouched by the fierce crosswind, it soared over one hundred yards and was still climbing. I gazed after it in total amazement; I remember thinking 'What a teacher I must be!' I turned to congratulate Mrs Noble, who at first was nowhere to be seen – until, that is, I looked down.

My first pupil was writhing on the ground, at first in silence, and then beginning to moan with pain. She was on her stomach, it was then that I realized that her left arm had come out of its socket and the huge bulge sticking up from her jersey was the upper end of her arm.

'Help me, help me,' she pleaded.

'I'm going for the doctor.'

'Don't go, it's so painful!'

Fortunately in my younger days my love for rugby football had taken me many times to Murrayfield, where we used to watch the great internationals. On one visit from the English, the great Melrose and Scotland winger Charlie Drummond had been brought down, probably by a late tackle, and was writhing about very close to the touchline where we were standing.

The one thing the English never really needed was a trainer; there always appeared to be so many on the pitch with medical degrees.

71

One such player, a doctor, diagnosed the situation immediately and got two colleagues to hold Charlie down, whilst he put one boot on his neck and the other into his rib-cage and then proceeded to pull the arm outwards to its maximum extent before releasing it with a bang, hoping that it would go into place.

Though this was unfortunate for Charlie, for I remember reading next day in the *Sunday Post* that he had only broken his collar bone, nevertheless I had the benefit of a first-class view of what to do in similar circumstances.

Mrs Noble, my first lady pupil, lay squirming on her stomach, so the job had to be done. First there were my new golf shoes, with gleaming half-inch spikes, to be got rid of, then I sat on the grass by her and put my left stockinged foot into her neck and my right into her rib-cage. I reached out for her wrist, which appeared to be coming out of the base of her neck.

'Oh God,' I remember thinking to myself, 'I hope this isn't going to happen every day.'

I pulled the arm through all the way, stretching my legs, until her knuckles touched my chin. She was now in total shock. Then I aimed, and let go. The arm seemed to bang back into its socket, and my pupil fainted.

I sat there, absolutely covered in perspiration, when, at that very moment, the Ladies' Captain, with other members of the team arrived around the gorse bush.

For a moment there was a stunned silence, then one of the ladies turned to her Captain and proclaimed. 'He's no different to all the others!' To which the Ladies' Captain, in defence of her decision that I was the man for the job replied, 'Yes he is, he's Scottish. At least he has the manners to take his boots off!'

13

THE 'CUSTOMER'S SHOT'

There are many great advantages when one progresses from Assistant to full Professional. In those days at East Herts I was given £200 annually as my retaining fee and provided with a lunch at half-price on those days when they did cater, and even though an hour's tuition there only bought ten shillings, it was all mine.

However, more important things happened; when I played in those marvellous winter Alliance meetings, I would be drawn with full professionals like Ronnie Mandeville, who served the West Herts Club for well over a quarter of a century. Dai Rees I played with often, also Bernard Hunt and John Jacobs, gentlemen from whom I learned a great deal.

In my very first spring I was asked to play in the annual match, the Hertfordshire Ladies verses the Professionals, a match which, no matter how hard we tried, we couldn't lose. The Ladies, though regular members of the County Amateur Side, simply got so uptight against the Professionals they fell apart.

My debut came at West Herts, and my partner was the ageing Alfie Hull, a lovely old man and professional at Knebworth, and from him I learned a new golfing expression, that of 'playing a customer's shot'.

We were playing foursomes, the two pros against the two ladies, each side sharing one ball by playing alternate shots – a form of golf more popular in historic times and known abroad as a 'Scotch Foursomes' – and the ladies were receiving a handicap of 6 shots, as well as a 4-up start. Everything possible was being done to let them beat us.

I have to admit that the elation of having been chosen was slightly dashed when the selectors later told me they had picked a team they hoped would lose. Nevertheless, I reached the 15th hole, and I was

73

playing exceptionally well and had made up for some of the strange shots Alfie had played, with the result that we were 3 up with only the four holes left.

Alfie had hit a strange drive that had hardly left the ground, and it only just reached the fairway, so much so that I had to walk back from where I stood, in anticipation, well down the fairway. The lady opponent I had waited with was happier, for her partner had struck a beauty, well past our ball.

I was preparing for the second shot to the green when I heard Alfie shuffling at some speed towards me: 'Hang on a minute, don't hit it yet.' I waited. Out of earshot from our opponents and gasping for breath he wheezed, 'Do me a favour and play a customer's shot.' This to me was a brand new expression and I looked at him somewhat perplexed. He went on, his face scarlet from the exertion: 'The one I'm driving against is my Ladies' Captain and we're beating them too much. She's already muttering that she's going to cancel the new set of clubs she has on order and probably her husband's too. We mustn't win, hit a customer's shot!'

'OK,' I agreed. 'What do I do?'

'Instead of hitting a no. 8 iron, take a no. 5 and hit it into the trees behind the green.'

I put the headcover back on my no. 4 wood.

Everything I had went into that iron shot, which flew like a bird and crashed into the dense forest well beyond the green.

Our opponents were lifted and the Ladies' Captain's partner hit a good shot on. 'Do I concede now Alfie?' My eagerness to complete my first customer's shot had carried me away. I had much to learn.

'No, a customer's shot has got to look genuine. We'll search for a while.'

We searched. 'I think the five minutes is up,' said the Ladies' Captain. 'We should claim the hole.'

I was about to agree when Alfie found our ball which, much to his relief, was in a ditch amongst the tree roots.

'We concede now?' I whispered to Alfie.

'No! With a customer's shot we make it look good.' The answer was whispered from the side of his mouth as he clambered into the ditch, sand-iron in his hand. At the top of his voice he called out to our opponents who had moved back on to the green, 'I'm going to play out wide.' They smiled confidently; they still had some handicap strokes to come and the 15th was surely now theirs.

Alfie, aiming at least fifty yards left of the green, still acting superbly, swung violently at the ball. He struck it with the socket of

the club so that, as in all true shanks, it left the club at right-angles. Next it struck a tree, from which it ricocheted still further right. Its next collision came half-way up the flag, from where it dropped gently into the hole.

Any chances Alfie's Ladies' Captain had of holing her putt were dashed by the tears in her eyes, and the match was over by 4 and 3.

We walked from there to the Clubhouse in a silent procession, until I turned to my partner, who was completely shattered.

'Alfie, if that's what you call a customer's shot, all I can say is you must have some awful good customers.'

14

———————•———————

MY FIRST ASSISTANT

Another feature of becoming the head Professional is that you can start employing Assistants, and looking back over the years I can recall many young men coming along, some making it to the playing ranks, others good professionals in clubs of their own, and inevitably others who either found the going too tough or simply found easier ways of making a living. Of those whose careers finished prematurely, I shall always have fond memories of my first Junior Assistant.

After a short time at the East Herts Club, when my wife was expecting our first child, it became necessary to engage an 'Aspro' (the abbreviation for Assistant Professional), since it had become impossible to cope with the large volume of lessons and still manage the shop.

The result of my advertisement was an application from one Christopher Hales. Chris was about six feet four inches tall, extremely well educated and obviously financially secure. My first reaction was that being a club- and shoe-cleaning junior shop assistant would not suit him at all; however, he was so keen, and he didn't want much money, so I took him on.

All worked fairly well, although it was fairly obvious that his night life was more important to him than his day-time activities; nevertheless, he was popular and his golf improved steadily.

There was nothing too strange about me arriving at the shop first and opening up, but one morning the phone rang and it was Mrs Hales: 'Poor Christopher,' Mummy explained 'has a dreadful cold and will not be able to work today.' This was most inconvenient, for I had a solid day's tuition booked and I knew there would be lots of golfers around requiring items from

76

the shop. Ann couldn't come in, for the baby was due any time.

I put a note on the door for clients to call me, and gave my lessons from a spot close to the shop, running in and out as required – definitely not the best method of teaching. Eventually the day was over and I went home exhausted and frustrated. Would 'poor Christopher' be in tomorrow, for I was just as heavily booked?

I was up bright and early and just had time to glance at the paper over breakfast before leaving for work. It was the William Hickey column, a gossip column running daily in the *Express*, that caught my eye. The tall, elegant, smiling young man in the photograph suddenly looked familiar. The caption read: 'The best dressed man at Royal Ascot yesterday was 19-year-old Christopher Hales, who appeared amongst the toppers and tails wearing a powder blue linen suit. Christopher is marking time between debutantes' parties as a golf professional in Hertfordshire.'

'Poor Christopher' was the first to work that morning; that was the day we parted company, a mutual decision being arrived at that he was in the wrong job.

Chris went off to the Stock Exchange, where he belonged, and joined Sunningdale, which was about right for him. He is there today, and very much involved with the world of horseracing as head of one of the leading gambling houses, City Index. Happily, we are very good friends, both having benefited from the short time we spent together.

———————●———————

As for the pupils, well once we had gotten over Mrs Noble, who not only improved and became the Ladies' Captain and also, together with her husband Leslie, the dearest of friends, I began to have some successes.

A little fellow, only twelve years of age, was brought along by his father for a weekly lesson. Being so tiny, he used to leap on to his toes with the effort of trying to hit the ball harder. I used to tell him that he would never be any good until he learned to be solid on his left heel at the moment he struck the ball.

I recall the comments made of him by the American Press at the Ryder Cup match at Laurel Valley in 1975, who claimed that 'Guy Hunt was the best striker of the ball in the British side, even

77

though he is on his toes when he hits it'. You can't be right all of the time.

The four years I spent at that little club are amongst my happiest. Many long lasting friendships were made there and marvellous memories too. But it was time to move up the ladder when the right job came along.

15

---•---

TOURNAMENT GOLF –
AND FRIENDS

One final advantage was that, as your own boss, you were free to enter into tournaments, but what an ill-prepared lot we were in those days! Unlike today's young professional players, who can move straight from the world of amateur golf, provided they gain a scratch handicap, to the qualifying rounds and so, if they score well enough, gain entry into the paid ranks.

Whilst it is not easy and great skill is required, at least there is no longer the need to spend several years as an apprentice in a shop. Poor Eric Brown who was one of Scotland's best ever: when he transferred from being a train-driver to being a professional golfer, the rules of the PGA forced him to spend five years as an assistant before permitting him to play in the major British events, even though he was winning international ones at the time.

For me it was a case of teaching all weekend to leave Ann with some money, driving off on Monday to the venue. Practice day was Tuesday, then Wednesday and Thursday saw the first two rounds, with the cut being made Thursday evening. The last two rounds were completed on the Friday, after which it was a race to get home, snatch some sleep and go teaching again next day.

I was very lucky to share driving with George Low, who was then an Assistant at the Enfield Club and a very talented player. In one three-week spell George finished 3rd, 2nd, and 3rd in top events and seemed on the verge of great things. I recall the Slazenger representative handing him as a reward a new golf bag to replace that of his contract, which was normally replaced every three years. The new one was plastic. Oh, how things have changed! Young men with only a fraction of the talent are today sponsored, driving about in company cars, dressed from head to toe in cashmere. George finally had to decide whether to go on or not and decided to give up and become a Club Professional, which he is happily today at Bush Hill Park Club, near Enfield. At least today we know that real talent is recognized and rewarded as it should be.

Another very good player I travelled and stayed with was Jimmy Hitchcock, who tried hard to help me with my play. Jimmy I had known since the Coombe Hill Assistants' Championship days, when he was the Assistant to Dick Burton and was known as one of the most dedicated young Professionals in the business.

Not being very tall, Jimmy had worked hard on his physical condition, with continual press-ups and other wrist exercises. He would start work early in the morning, cleaning out the Professional's Shop whilst it was still dark, so that he might gain from the boss an extra hour of practice during the daylight hours.

It was when he was out hitting more balls that the other Assistants decided to play a trick on him. In those days every professional's shop had an old stoneware varnish pot which, when left overnight used to seal itself so that it required some strength to prise it open next day. As Jimmy set off for the practice ground the others put the already sticking lid into the vice and twisted the pot even more anti-clockwise until it was completely jammed; then they left the varnish to harden.

When Jimmy returned, they made a great fuss about the pot being unopenable, challenging him to get the lid off, accusing him of having been last to replace it. Of course his first efforts proved unsuccessful, until, summoning up his full strength, he applied his fingers to the lid and twisted. The lid didn't turn; instead the top half of the stone pot sheared off from the bottom clean as a whistle.

It was his dedication that cost Jimmy his first full professional position at Verulam Golf Club near St Albans. Instead of giving lessons and selling balls, he was out hitting thousands of them every day. So many in fact that for years the trench on the practice area which he had dug himself into was there for all to see.

His greatest success was winning the old Dunlop Masters when it was played at Sunningdale, which incidentally he did using the same ball for all four rounds. It was a Dunlop ball which he felt flew so well that he just kept using it each day. His greatest disappointment was failing to be picked for the Ryder Cup Team when all his performances suggested he should have been; I don't think he has ever got over that.

His efforts to help me included my staying at his apartment over his professional's shop at Ashford Manor Golf Club. First, I had to improve my diet; this was done by eating near-raw steaks and uncooked vegetables. Next was my mental attitude, to gain power of positive thought, coupled with the ability to relax.

Each evening during London-based tournaments his wife would prepare these excellent meals; whilst she did, Jimmy would squeeze a damp towel, one of the best finger-strengthening exercises I've ever come across. After dinner he would read to me from a book called *Relax and Live*. This treatment he first applied when, after a disappointing opening round on the West at Wentworth, I knew I had to do a good one next day on the East.

As instructed, I lay back on the couch and pictured a huge black sheet hanging on a line. His idea was that you concentrate on the sheet, forgetting the line, until you could picture all black. This you added to by long, slow deep breathing exercises, and within minutes you would be totally relaxed.

When I left him next morning on Wentworth's putting green and headed for the first on the East, I promised I would apply the technique, being careful to warn my caddie, for he would certainly think I was in some sort of a trance. I did not wish him even to speak to me until the round was over, and this he faithfully promised to do.

I stood on the tee waiting to be announced, my black sheet billowing on its line; my name was called. I breathed deeply. I was totally relaxed, my tee shot astonished everyone on the tee, none more than my caddie. It split the centre of the fairway, carrying the road easily.

I walked along, guided by the blurred sound of my irons rattling in the bag. My 7-iron second never left the flag, the ball pitching just beyond the hole and running four yards past.

Again the caddie guided me towards the green; I felt as though I was floating. My putt just slid by, and a safe par was scored.

My tee-shot down the hill at the 2nd was another cracker. My black sheet was flooding my mind. The iron shot pitched right by the hole and stopped stone-dead. I was aware of tapping the ball in one-handed, something I had never dared to do under competition circumstances.

Across the gulley at the 3rd, those cross-bunkers that had previously worried me were not given a thought; my drive was still climbing as it took the longest carry. The rugged footpath from tee to fairway was covered by me, one hand on the bottom of my bag, my caddie leading me like a survivor of a First World War gas attack.

By now my deep breathing was putting so much oxygen in my lungs I was feeling quite lightheaded; still my black sheet was intact.

The second shot, a full-blooded wedge, was struck just at the moment Tom Haliburton, playing with the Argentine ace Antonio Cerda and on the 4th tee, was about to start his backswing. At the point where he reached the top of the swing my ball plunged full-toss into the hole for an eagle 2. This was witnessed by hundreds who were following him and who all roared at the same instant. Tom's shot missed the short hole green by miles, and he glared towards me. I was too relaxed to notice, I was surrounded by my black sheet.

It was on the next tee that unfortunately my caddie broke his vow of silence. 'Blimey Guv, what's bleedin 'appenin' 'ere? 'Ole this an' you'll be in the bleedin' *Guinness Book of Records*. Four, three, two, bleedin' one, that ain't bin done before.'

My clothes line broke, my black sheet blew away. I shanked my 5 iron and took 6.

As for Jimmy, well some years later his black sheet blew away too. It happened at the Villa d'Este in the Italian Open where he had held the course record with 61. At the 9th green, partnering Belgian's Flory Van Donck, he stood over a putt. There had been a growing suspicion that his putting touch was becoming edgy, and the signs of the dreaded putting twitch were growing evident, the time spent over each putt getting longer.

That particular green was very soft, there had been heavy overnight rain, and Jimmy was over the ball. Minutes later he was still over it; he was completely stationary. There was no movement at all, not that is except from the ball, which rolled backwards and settled on top of the putter head. Jimmy's increasing weight as he tilted more and more forward had driven the putter deeper and deeper into the green, where the ball toppled back on top of it.

It was Flory who first realized his partner's nerve had gone; he walked over, took Jimmy's putter from him and quietly led him from the course to the Clubhouse.

Jimmy left the world of tournament golf and emigrated to South Africa, where he became a most successful and popular Club Professional. No doubt many of his pupils have applied the black sheet treatment.

16

---•---

THE FINAL TOURNAMENT

It was at Wentworth, in the old DAK's tournament, that my decision was made to part company with the tournament scene and become a teacher; that is what you do if you can't play; if you're not too hot at teaching you can write books and magazine articles; if your English isn't too hot then the BBC will probably grab you. That was how my career was once described when being introduced at a dinner as a guest speaker.

Without the finance to spare for hotels I was commuting to Wentworth in our old car. Thanks to making a hole in one at the 14th – that tricky one up the hill on which I often commentate and would dearly love to tell the world as the superstars take 3s and 4s at it, but modesty forbids me – I had made the cut and was due to tee off with fellow-Scot, George Will, an up and coming player. Ann and I had discussed my continuance at this costly business and it was decided that, should I make money in this event, I would continue; if not, I would retire and teach.

My car had a puncture just outside Staines and I couldn't get the wheel off, with the result that I arrived, driving right up behind the first tee, late. The starter, Donald Ross had already replaced me with a marker and George had just driven.

'You're disqualified for being late.'

I explained to Donald, adding the decision my wife and I had made in the hope of some sympathy. I showed my oily palms.

'Let him play,' said George. 'The marker hasn't driven yet.'

Donald studied the watch. 'OK, if you go now.'

'I'll get changed,' I said, pulling my clubs and shoes from the car.

'No time for that, hit it or you're out.'

Good old George had actually teed up a ball for me to save time. 'C'mon,' he said, 'hit this one quickly.'

I remember those next minutes vividly. It was pouring with rain, the grass was soaking. I pulled the driver from the bag and stepped over the fence. I recall, as I swung, my casual moccasin-style slip-on shoes slipping. I can see to this day the ball veering left in a driving hook towards what is now Bernard Gallagher's shop, then Tom Haliburton's, then seeing it ricochet back from the wall, clearing those Professionals who hadn't already scattered from its first pass from the putting green, to disappear finally by the large clump of rhododendron just beyond the putting green.

'Keep your head,' said my helpful partner. 'You're still level par.'

By now I'd got my shoes changed and passed my car keys to a friend to park it, and they had found me a caddie.

This caddie was one of that old brigade, a cockney who was sleeping rough, dirty and smelly. You hardly see their like today, for caddies are progressing rapidly into recognition. The ancient overcoat, with the wrong buttons done up so that one side hung below the other, the soggy *Sporting Life* sticking out of one pocket. It has always fascinated me how you'll often see at a prosperous golf club some toff get out of his Bentley, dressed in his twills and cashmeres, and call out to one of these caddies, 'Got a tip for me today, Charlie?' Surely if Charlie was such an expert he too would be in a Bentley!

The 'Charlie' who was now carrying my bag was grumbling at having been wakened up before the effect of the previous evening's beverage had worn off. Already the rain was dripping down his neck, and his thick glasses, one earpiece missing, were covered in raindrops.

We located the ball. Charlie had no idea where it had gone; he was obviously deaf as well as blind, otherwise he would have heard its crash against the wall, or even the cries from those ducking and diving from its path. It lay just at the base of the bush, close to a fairly thick stem. One thing that a professional golfer should have gained over years of playing is the power of positive thinking. Had I benefited from those years, then the decision would have been straightforward. A wedge-shot back to the fairway, a wood towards the green, a chip and a putt. Wentworth's first was a par 5 in those days.

'Give me my 3 wood.' I had not learned! Nor had Charlie, for he gave it to me without argument. The result was that the shaft of my favourite club caught the protruding stem and snapped. Somehow the clubhead, now on its own, caught the ball, which shot upwards and forwards a considerable distance, but even wider off the fairway. Charlie was tutting – the very last thing you need at a time like that is a critical caddie.

'Well, it's bloody difficult,' was all I could say to him.

'Listen son, if you ever get it on grass, you can have a free drop.' He had at last found something funny to say; I didn't like the joke.

We progressed up the hole, George cracking a sweet 3-iron shot to the very heart of the green. My ball lay not too badly but still about 150 yards from the green.

'Can I make it with a 7 iron?' I asked, staring at the distant green. Charlie's sense of humour had gone once again; the walk through the deep, wet rough had already penetrated the ancient and cracked black and white Lotus shoes which he had inherited after a locker-room clearout some years before.

'How many times are you going to hit it?' That crack cheered him up a little, then he introduced the 'do you down' tactics the Wentworth caddies are renowned for. Anyone who has experienced this will have been told how his caddie used to work for Big Jack, or Lee, or some other household name.

Such information is usually given as you reach for your wallet to pay him. In this instance Charlie was introducing his strategy early, on the opening hole.

'Arnie hit a nine iron from here,' was all he said.

Now I was mad, and certainly not thinking straight, otherwise I might have asked him what the devil Arnie had been doing here. Instead I grabbed the 9 iron from the bag and prepared to hit, adding all the devices of a shot that is to be forced. The stance was wide, with the right side drawn back, the right hand removed from the delicate finger-grip into the brutal palm position, and then I launched at the ball. It soared to the right and then, as my modifications took effect, it commenced its homing-in towards the green.

Those who have either played Wentworth or watched it on television will recall a large deep bunker, just short and right of the green. My full-blooded 9-iron shot buried in its face.

'Ain't it funny?' laughed Charlie. 'That's where Arnie went.'

After what seemed like a lifetime I completed the hole in 7; George had made a birdie 4, and we moved to the second tee. My heart wasn't in it, I didn't even observe the big Scot's iron to the flag. Although it is illegal, George passed me and whispered, 'That was a 7 iron. Now pull yourself together, you're only 2 over!'

I thanked him and reached towards my bag, when the huge, grubby, nicotine-stained hand gripped my wrist. Charlie leaned over to me, the wet fag-end which he'd managed to find time to roll whilst I was hacking about in the sand hanging soggy from the side of his mouth, his red eyes peering at me over the top of the thick lenses. 'Listen Guv'nor, I've caddied in Pro-Ams before, you ignore what them Pros is using.' I was dumbfounded. Charlie coughed, spat, then continued, 'I've assessed your swing – you take a 4 wood!'

'Listen,' I responded, 'the hole's 153 yards!'

Charlie released his grip on my wrist, lifted his glasses up on his nose and peered through the rain-spotted lenses towards the green.

'You're quite right, Guv'nor, 'ere take the driver.'

I took my no. 6 iron and duffed it short of the green. That was my last tournament, and I became a teacher, no doubt much to Charlie's relief.

17

---●---

DUNHAM FOREST

Because of the great surge in golf course construction, many Professionals will be given the opportunity that came my way not once, but twice, that of being the Club Professional at a brand-new club. Though this can primarily be a costly experience, especially for those who are already in good positions at well-established clubs, there is the advantage of being in residence as the membership builds, when good business relationships may be struck up from the outset and many happy associations formed.

When I say 'costly', I refer to a fact many don't appreciate, that, unlike selling up a high street shop and its 'goodwill', no matter how well a Professional develops his business at a golf club, the day he decides to leave, or the day when the Club Committee decides he should, he has nothing to sell. In many cases he is told not even to have a sale of his stock in case that might spoil trade for the next incumbent.

When I left East Herts and went north to the soon-to-be-opened Dunham Forest, though I was going from a fairly small turnover business I felt that the risk was worthwhile and I had my ladder to climb. Besides having been apprenticed at a Jewish Golf Club, which is what Dunham was, I felt certain of good support.

Years later, leaving Ashridge for Woburn was a different matter, for Ashridge, the gem of Hertfordshire, which was made famous by Henry Cotton, who won Open Championships playing from there, is where I had spent twelve happy years and had developed an excellent business.

On reflection, leaving such security, and with nothing to sell, to move into a nine-foot caravan parked behind a log-cabin temporary clubhouse, knowing there would be no retail income for nearly a year until the Clubhouse and Shop were built, requiring my stock to be packed into storage crates, I think I can understand why so many said I was mad.

Perhaps I was lucky, or perhaps I had the vision to see that Woburn had the international future I wanted to be involved in; the prestige of its owners, the Marquess of Tavistock and Rothmans International, was as good as any written guarantee to me. Besides I had already had my judgement tested at Dunham Forest, where the twenty or so members who founded it had nothing to offer me but their fantastic enthusiasm; they didn't even have a log cabin.

Dunham has fulfilled those early dreams and is established as one of the leading clubs in the north of England and I wouldn't have missed the experience of those early primitive days, for their dream was mine too. Virtually teaching an entire membership to play golf, often being on the teaching strip for eleven hours a day, earned me many friends and taught me a great deal.

I was interviewed for the position of Professional at this brand new Jewish Club whilst it was being built on the land belonging to Lord Stamford, on the outskirts of Altrincham in Cheshire; and, since the course was only just seeded, permission was given by neighbouring Ringway Golf Club for interviews and playing examinations to be carried out there.

Unfortunately on the morning in question a thick fog shrouded the area and visibility on the course was about fifty yards. Nevertheless the Committee wanted to see me in action: my training at Potter's Bar had obviously stood me in good stead, but could I play?

The club's first Captain, Harry Doniger, and future Captains, Sydney Woolf and Arnold Wills, made up the four. On the 1st tee they pointed out a spot twenty yards ahead, which was only just visible, and told me to drive over it, which I did. All of their balls got lost, mine was in the centre of the fairway. A no. 7 iron was suggested, to be aimed just left of what looked like a bunker a few yards ahead. We found the ball only two yards from the hole.

Nine holes were played, and the furthest that I finished from any flag was about four yards. They were astounded; so was I, for I had never played that well before and certainly never since. The job was mine.

Ann and our son Graeme were packed off to Musselburgh, for we had no home of our own, then I, together with my assistant, set off to seek our fortune in the North. Bob White was his name, a very big lad who could hit the ball a long way and who had a wonderful way with the ladies. One of life's likeable rogues, who when I last heard of him was sailing a small ferry boat amongst the islands off the north-west coast of Scotland. Hopefully they lock up the sheep at night up there.

We had been promised a well-appointed shop with a forty-foot showroom; this turned out to be a Second World War pre-fab salvaged from demolition in Glasgow. Like most things salvaged from Glasgow, it was incomplete, having no gutters, so the rain ran down the corrugated roof and then dropped inside the walls rather than outside. It was also without window catches, which meant it could not be sealed. Not that windows made a lot of difference, as we were to find out later.

A delivery van followed us north, and we unloaded the results of the past four years efforts into the building. We piled everything up in the centre of the floor away from the puddles, and got on with making a shop.

Obviously we couldn't leave the premises, which were set deep in the forest (we named the building 'Mellor's Place' after that of Lady Chatterley's lover). So at night I would drive to Altrincham and bring back fish and chips, and we slept in sleeping-bags on the floor.

This is no criticism of Dunham Forest, for they had no clubhouse, just about twenty-five enthusiasts with a dream which they have realized and which I am very proud to have been a part of. That pre-fab was divided in half and provided a showroom for me on the right and, somehow, a club- and shoe-storage area, a workshop and a changing room in the other half.

Some members rallied round, and we had the windows welded closed and encased in wire mesh. A heavy felt was substituted for the gutters so the water could run down the outside walls. The Dunlop company came in and fitted floor tiles for me, and we were in business.

Not all were helpful – one in particular, who had such a great love for his Cheshire that he wanted us to paint our pre-fab white then add black painted beams, so that it would resemble the Tudor style of the best homes in the area, similar to that which he lived in. Another was a Scottish Insurance Broker who managed to arrange insurance cover for the shop at great expense to me after I had begged him to persuade the Committee that a new shop be the first priority in the new building, which had now been started. Instead he persuaded Lloyds in London to take the risk, which they did after I had been forced to install a loud burglar-alarm system, again at my expense.

My plea to him, which was of no avail, had come after our first break-in, which had been accomplished by means of a half-inch spanner and simply undoing the bolts which held the wall together, then removing a panel.

Unfortunately for our thief, as he reached in, he knocked over a club, which, as it fell, broke the beam of the 'magic eye' and set

89

off the bells. He had also come through where the racks of clubs were assembled and could not gain proper entry. As he struggled to squeeze through the gap, his British Rail cap was dislodged and it rolled into the room and out of his reach. He grabbed a lovely new set of Wilson clubs and made off into the night.

The Cheshire constabulary were confident. All they had to do was find the railway worker who had lost his hat; unfortunately at that time 75% were hatless, so I assume he and his ill-gotten gains lived happily ever after.

However, the police were extremely unhappy at the vulnerability, as well as at the danger of getting through the forest to the shop, which could only be accomplished on foot. They made an official complaint, which delighted me: surely now we would have a new shop. My Scottish friend came up with yet another solution, a dog.

Bob and I were taken by an RSPCA official to their kennels. After all, there was no use in getting a puppy and training it; besides they had just the dog for us, one which would scare thieves away.

How right they were: this was not so much a dog as a man-eater. It greeted our approach when we were about twenty yards from the cage by hurling itself, snarling and clawing, at the wire to get at us.

'He'll be ideal for you,' said our official pulling on steel mesh gloves. 'Once you've had him a few days he'll grow to love you.' I recall wondering which part of me. 'Until then we'll lend you this chain.'

He produced a twenty-foot length of inch-wide linked chain with a huge studded collar attached. 'Raw meat is the best.' The dog was making that abundantly clear.

They delivered Tiddles (that's what Bob named it, in memory of a cat he once owned) on Monday morning; they felt that after a busy weekend we would have five days to become close friends before the next weekend's flood of members arrived. They also left us with a few days' supply of raw meat cut up into small pieces so that we could throw it to him until it was safe to approach. Then, before detaching the muzzle, tugging it off with a long pole, they attached the chain to a vice on the solid workbench. No repairs were done for some time.

The first day was terrifying; even approaching the shop set the beast snarling and clawing at the floors and the walls to get at us, but we persisted. We threw it pieces of meat regularly, and surprisingly enough the RSPCA man was right: by day two we could actually approach and feed it by hand. After two days we took it out for exercise, both of us keeping a tight hold of the chain, for it went beserk at anything that moved and no one person could control the monster.

Behind the shop we built a great kennel close to a large pine to which we were able to fasten the twenty-foot chain and so get on with our work.

At that time some regular caddies were attaching themselves to the Club, for work was plentiful. One, Jock was his name (he is still around surprisingly enough, and he and I still meet regularly at tournaments, for he is a current tour caddie), reckoned himself an authority on dogs. It proved to be a pity that the dogs didn't know this, for though we told him to keep away he felt he knew better.

Unfortunately the moment he chose was after the morning's play the very next Sunday. Tiddles was safely fastened to the tree and lay, out of the sun, growling quietly in the kennel. The shop was packed, on Sundays, at around lunchtime it was not a pretty place to be. Members of all shapes and sizes changed shoes, socks, slacks, even underwear in the changing area. On this particular day, which was extremely hot, clothes and bodies and, of course, arguments were abundant.

It was at that moment Jock, deciding the Pros were too busy to notice, chose to become acquainted with our latest means of keeping our insurance cover. He was exactly twenty-one feet from the kennel when our monster vacated it. Horizontal the beast was, heading for the throat, when the twenty-foot chain ran out. The force was such that the chain snapped in three places, but fortunately it had succeeded in slowing the momentum, and so the dog missed Jock's throat and instead collided with his chest. Jock passed out.

In total panic, and free for the first time for months, Tiddles raced for the workshop, heading for his bed, which was kept under the bench in the changing room.

His claws slipped on the highly polished Dunlop floor-tiles as he cornered through the showroom, and he crashed amongst the membership, most of whom had not been previously introduced to the beast.

Who was frightened the most I know not, but the dog was snarling and frothing, and the fastest exodus in history was made as my clientele scattered through the door and up the hill, some dressed, most not, underpants and bare bums everywhere.

In every crisis one man stands above the others. That day it was Sydney Woolf, who positioned himself by our confectionery counter unwrapping Mars bars and throwing them to the hound. He saved the day, but took care to throw the last one from the doorway as he joined his colleagues.

Next morning I was instructed to attend an extraordinary Committee meeting, which took place on the hill fifty yards from the shop,

and where it was decided that Tiddles had to go and that a new shop would be built.

The sequel to the story is a strange one, for the RSPCA telephoned to say that whilst Tiddles had been in our possession *she* had become pregnant. We had never been close enough to establish the sex, and how she got in that state I'll never know.

The construction of the course at Dunham was no easy matter, and it is hard to believe when you look at the beautiful course the members now enjoy just how many difficulties the founder-members faced, not the least of which was the owner of the land, Lord Stamford, who, to put it in the mildest terms, was a bit eccentric.

He called himself a tree-lover and used this as an excuse to insist that trees, even those of no significance, must be left in certain places even though they rendered the completion of a hole out of the question. In one instance, a tee was built on the only possible site for it, which had a tree growing at the front end of it. His Lordship, though happy to enjoy the revenue, was not interested in the fact that a golf course cannot be built without the removal of some trees, so the tree stayed. It remained until the very day he became the late Lord Stamford, when it became the late pussy-willow.

Another problem came from the fact that the land had been used as a prisoner-of-war camp to detain German soldiers, and was littered with the concrete bases upon which their huts had stood. Those that faced the right direction were earthed over and became tees; the rest had to be dug out and removed.

A huge reservoir was also being built on the land, which, when completed and roofed over, became part of the course. It actually turned out to be the only golf course I have ever fallen off! I took a nasty tumble from the top in the early days before the turf had taken, and nearly broke an ankle.

The first year of play required members to use tee-pegs for every shot, other than bunker shots and putts, for the grass was young and very thin. About six months into the Club's life a group of members decided to have a day out and take the Professionals with them. Stockport Golf Club was chosen, especially renowned for its superb lush green fairways, and always in tip-top condition. Fortunately the competition we played that day was only for fun; most of the group would have been disqualified on the opening hole when they automatically picked their ball up from the fairway, wiped it clean and proceeded to tee it up before realizing this was illegal.

I was partnering one of the Club's great characters, Archie Preston, soon to be one of the early Captains, when his ball lay about a hundred yards from the 1st green. Archie stood there looking down upon his brilliant white Dunlop 65 sitting up on the bristling green sward; he was, unusually for him, in a silent trance.

This was broken by the caddie, who clattered the bag down on its end; he pulled a 9 iron from the bag: 'Take this sir, and don't force it.'

Archie didn't look up but said, 'Gimme my brassie.'

'Your brassie?' The caddie was now reaching the conclusion that many of Archie's pals had claimed for many years past. 'You must be mad. The green's only a hundred yards away. Your brassie'll go half way down the next hole.'

'Never mind that,' said Archie. 'gimme the brassie, I haven't had a lie like this for six months!'

18

---•---

LE TOUQUET

Joining Dunham Forest introduced me to many lasting friends and great characters – none more so than one real eccentric by the name of David Norton, whose family had prospered in the great steel-mill days of Salford in Lancashire.

David lived in a mansion alongside what we then played as the 5th of the original nine holes that opened. At first we wondered about him, for though he'd joined the Club we hadn't seen him, besides, his was a staunch Catholic family. What we did see every Sunday morning was the 5th fairway adjacent to the house, littered with broken eggs.

David claimed himself to be one of the great egg-throwers, his skill dating back to his schooldays at Eton, who was capable of throwing an egg across the roof of his house and landing it unbroken at the other side. From the debris it was obvious that he was losing his touch, for his destruction of eggs has only been rivalled by Edwina Currie.

David, whose love for throwing eggs was only equalled by his love of champagne (which led him regularly to 'the dog house', as Monique, his fairly excitable French wife, banished him) introduced me to golfing abroad.

The Nortons had a lovely home in Le Touquet and David would move over there every August to join Monique and their children, who spent the summer in France. The two glorious golf courses and Le Touquet itself were, in those days, at an 'in-between' stage. Gone were the days when the rich English aristocracy would motor to the south coast and catch the channel packet to spend their summers at L'Hermitage or in their own magnificent homes. First the Germans had stopped that in 1939, and the RAF had removed L'Hermitage and the Clubhouse from the face of the earth a few years later.

Then, finally, the progress of air travel brought the South of France, with its better climate, into range, and the area became French again.

Now there is a resurgence of golfing Britishers, as well as other Europeans, visiting Le Touquet, and the area which was glaringly ripe for development is turning into a golfing Mecca.

In 1960 it was possible for David and his friends to walk straight onto the first tee of La Mer at any time of the day, whilst the French, who found that marvellous links much too daunting, queued in droves to play the shorter Forêt course.

On those glorious August days, when I became an annual house guest, it was a joy to play on one of Europe's best link courses. We were always joined at the 9th green by Monsieur Charles, a charming man who loved the place and had started his working life as a junior barman in the old Clubhouse and now ran Le Manoir, a superb building used as a clubhouse and restaurant, and who would drive his car along a well-worn track out across the dunes with two bottles of champagne and a tray of smoked salmon sandwiches in a hamper tucked in the boot. This would sustain us until we were safely back at Le Manoir for lunch.

Monique suggested it would be a good idea to have a birthday tea for Christopher, her eldest son, who would be twelve, and ask Le Manoir's chef to bake a special birthday cake big enough to feed an army of nephews and nieces (her whole family used to descend on Le Touquet for the summer). David, she suggested, should order this, after we had completed our round of golf for the following day; this he did, but omitted to point out to Charles that the large birthday cake was for his son and not for himself.

I shall never forget Charles' expression when the cars spilled out the hordes of children on to the steps of Le Manoir, which was matched moments later when the chef appeared around the kitchen door and found out this was a children's party and not one for David's normal colleagues. David was immediately taken to one side, where it was explained to him that the cake was definitely an adult's cake and certainly not a children's cake. Assurances were given by David, who was eyeing up the work of art on its silver platter, that this was no problem; neither the chef nor Charles would be held responsible. What's more, David claimed, 'So long as no one tells Monique the difference will never be noticed.'

The chef rolled his eyes.

The first suggestion that this statement was not totally accurate came when Monique asked the Head Waiter if someone had spilled some brandy at lunch time in the room, which she claimed, reeked of it. The second came when a six-year-old cousin, midway through her first portion of cake, toppled from her chair to the floor, out for the count.

'Poor thing,' said David, 'she's tired out.' Turning to the child's mother: 'You French keep children up too late at night!'

That certainly proved to be correct that evening, for almost the entire group spent most of it in their various toilets being sick.

Our cake was completely devoured, mainly by the fathers, who had reluctantly given a sporting afternoon to attend with their offspring and were now enthusiastically tucking in. What a blessing there were no breathalysers then, no one would have passed the test.

David was returned to the dog house!

With Bill Shankland at Potters Bar, one of the best players never to win The Open. He came so close. Nevertheless as a teacher and as a man he had few equals.

Going for it with the brassie in the Boys' Championship.

How things have changed! Henry Cotton in his overcoat teaching, with the caddie about to tee up the next ball. Behind the lovely thatched clubhouse of Ashridge; with 'Cottons' ninth green to the right.

(Top left) Not the place one expects to be giving lessons, the practice-ground at the Ryder Cup. Howard Clark had lost form and looked like being out of the match. By the final day his form was back and he was selected. A proud moment for him when the team 'went up'.

(Bottom left) Young Paul Way in the happy days of his professional career. Maybe success came too easy. Next time he will be here to stay!

(Above) Making the really funny men laugh, or even just smile, is an achievement. Johnny Riscoe, the dog fancier, and Jimmy Tarbuck at a Variety Club dinner.

(Right) Reminding Tony, as he was coming to the end of his competitive days, that the older you get the shallower the clubface should be. He has the odd grey hair too. What joy he brought to all of us at Lytham in 1969.

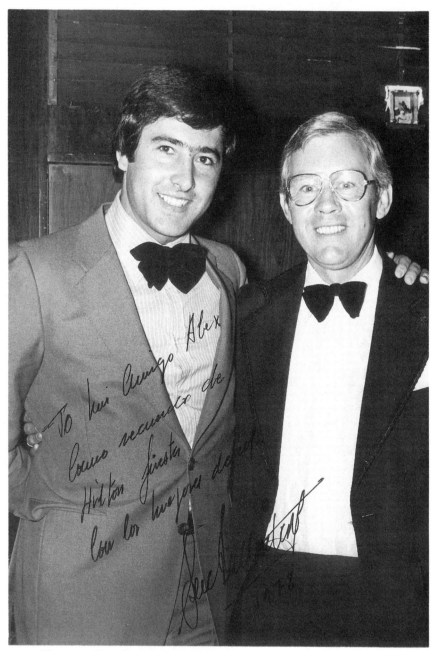

*The young Seve, he turned up with the wrong suit, borrowed a tie from the
head waiter, and got a standing ovation.*

With Tony Jacklin, recalling some of the humorous times at Potters Bar.

Woburn has enjoyed many of the world's great players. On this occasion Gary Player was matched against Seve Ballesteros. John Jacobs was the referee.

Working with Peter Alliss, the man who possesses the fastest reaction to a humorous situation I've ever met, reduces me to fits of laughter that bring my commentary to a halt.

The BBC commentary team. No, I am not taller than Peter Alliss, I just happened to be standing on a roll of television cable. Bruce Critchley, Clive Clark, Peter Alliss, Alex Hay, Harry Carpenter.

The commentary box at Dubai where Renton Laidlaw and I felt like two legionnaires.

Not all commentary boxes are as luxurious as viewers imagine. Getting up this one in Hong Kong was terrifying – coming down even more so.

Yours truly in full swing.

19

---•---

BASTILLE NIGHT

Our longest and most serious visit to the dog house, for I was now adjudged to be an accomplice, since most trouble appeared to occur that week when I was present, came on a Bastille Night. A celebration dinner-dance was to be held in that marvellous restaurant Flavio's, which no one who visits Le Touquet should ever miss, at which full evening dress would be worn.

There can be nowhere in the world to equal France when it comes to glamorous parties. The place was full of beautiful, elegant and sophisticated women accompanied by debonair companions, and the champagne flowed, dangerous for the dynamic duo from across the Channel, especially when the subject turned to rugby football, for which both David and I had a great passion.

The merits of French, English and Scottish styles of play were bandied about. Who had the best technique for passing a rugby ball was to be proved by David, who, as part of his demonstration, positioned me at one end of the room by the staircase, whilst he made a passage through the highly amused clientele along which a melon might travel uninterrupted.

Monsieur Flavio didn't like it – not surprisingly, I suppose, for, though I caught the first one easily, I missed the second owing to a perfect interception by an agile, handsome Frenchman, which brought cheers from the audience but not from David, who had now reduced them to 'Bloody Frogs' and claimed that the interception had been offside, typically French. The dog house was looming, Monique becoming furious.

Flavio suggested we settle this outside, and then unfortunately a 'Froggy' who knew of David's prowess called out that melons were the wrong shape: 'Get him some eggs.'

Anything, thought Monsieur Flavio, to get us out of the building, and I was handed a cardboard tray of one dozen eggs. I would be David's second. Out we went onto the pavement opposite the rolling lawns of the spectactulary lit-up Westminster Hotel.

With David, myself and our main rivals safely outside the restaurant, and even though others hung out of the windows to spectate, Monsieur Flavio got his Bastille Evening under way again; the band struck up and the dancing began, that awful French dancing where they do a sort of circle waltz but at high speed, all building up to a frenzied climax. They keep it up for hours; it is so painful on the calf muscles.

Outside on that balmy evening, oblivious of the noise of the orchestra, David was informing the French of his opinions of them – even their capitulation in 1940 was not left out – and was now offering to take bets of one thousand francs an egg that he could land them on the Westminster Hotel lawn without them breaking.

We had several takers for the first egg. David carefully selected the missile from the tray which I held out at arms length before him; it was a white one and, since David was an expert, this dispelled my belief that brown shells were tougher.

Taking up his Etonian stance, feet well apart, left shoulder high in front of the chin, a bit like Peter Thomson's address position, he turned the egg gently in his fingers until his forefinger rested on the pointed end and his thumb beneath the rounded.

Even the frenzied music appeared to die, the French were silent, the egg arched through those high street-lamps, easily carrying the floral displays, in a beautiful perfect curve, flying as though in slow motion. I remember a feeling of pride in knowing such a genius. Then it landed and it bounced, once twice and thrice, and came to a halt by the feet of the Westminster's astonished doorman.

The pavement was emptying, those French who thought they would escape their bets were joining their partners on the floor. Then one, hanging from the window, made his biggest mistake by calling out in English, 'They're china eggs!'

'Oh, they are, are they?' David wrenched from my hands the tray containing the other eleven and hurled the lot through the window, the space now vacated by our critic. The eleven fresh eggs made it all the way to the dance floor just at the moment the orchestra reached its frenzied climax, arriving with complete indiscrimination.

David and I were well and truly in the dog house!

20

THE CASINO

Just across the main street from Flavio's stands the magnificent Casino, where it used to be compulsory that evening dress was worn; indeed it probably clung to its dress standards longer than most casinos.

This was my very first experience of a gambling house, and I used to watch David at play, often winning or losing in an evening sums of money that I would have been happy to earn in a year.

Personally I have never been a gambler, though I have been fairly successful at picking the winners of Open Championships, my greatest success being at Sandwich, when I selected America's Bill Rodgers to win and the young Bernhard Langer to be placed, which was how they finished. In a casino I always allow myself about £25 and when it goes, as it always does, I stop.

On my first visit to Le Touquet David was busy at the roulette table and doing well when I joined him; I had been wandering around clutching my stock of plastic chips, not even certain how to place a bet, studying the technique of the experts, who were normally elderly French widows whose husbands had worked their way into the grave, leaving them to dispose of the assets. David introduced me to the croupier, who sat on a high chair overlooking and supervising play. In French he told him that I was new and needed looking after, then whispered to him something I didn't hear. The croupier, never taking his eyes once from the table, nodded in agreement.

'Pierre will tell you what to put your money on, do nothing until then.'

I remember wondering if the croupier would do that for me then why wasn't David waiting for his advice? I stood close to my new financial adviser, full of wonder for his skill and mathematical

99

brain; the speed at which they sweep bets onto the various parts of the table, and the ability to remember who placed what where, then the swiftness of the scoop that gathers up the losers' stakes, is truly a work of art. As far as I knew, neither of us could speak the other's language, so I waited silently.

Then it happened, he turned to me and whispered just one word: 'Deux'. I placed the equivalent of half my gambling allowance on the table and slid the little heap towards Pierre so that he could sweep it into position, and then, in my near-perfect French, and so that no one would think this was a conspiracy, I announced boldly, 'Deux.' With only the merest of acknowledgement, Pierre guided my money safely into position in the centre of DEUX, and I returned to the chairside to await the outcome.

Around went the wheel, then the little ball; it seemed to roll longer than ever; finally it stopped. 'Deux!' Amidst the sighs and moans of the losers – mine was the only bet on DEUX – a huge collection of little towers of chips was swept across the table and placed immediately before me.

I thought to myself, 'This isn't a bad place to stand.' I could get awfully rich here. Then my Scottish upbringing took over; this was no time to take risks. I divided my new wealth into two piles and put the first into my pockets in case of a rainy day, as my mother always trained me to do; the other slid towards Pierre in readiness for our next play. I recall Pierre, even though his training as a croupier permitted no change of facial expression, looking just a little surprised. Was I being greedy? Perhaps I should wait patiently for his further instructions. The answer came swiftly.

'Merci, Monsieur.' His smile beamed down at me, and with one flick of the wrist, manipulating his scoop, my pile of chips was swept down the slot of his tip box!

I had suddenly become the last of the big tippers. Then Pierre leaned over and said in perfect English, 'You will be welcome here, Monsieur, at any time.'

21

HARRY BENTLEY

Another who had enjoyed no mean share of the bright lights but who was now trying to give it all up was Harry Bentley, a former English international golfer and extremely successful businessman who had a villa overlooking the 13th green on the Sea Course.

Like David, Harry was married to a charming French lady, also named Monique, and she too spent most of her time trying to keep a wild, sporting, fast-living Englishman under control. Since Harry had promised to give up drinking many times and failed an equal amount, Monique had found a possible solution. On the highly polished hall table stood a bottle of Scotch whisky and a single crystal glass, beside which lay an opened cheque book and a fountain pen. The first cheque was already filled in – except, that is, for the signature. It was made out to Monique for £1,000, and all Harry had to do in order to open the bottle and pour himself a drink was to sign his name.

Every August the final game of my week's holiday was over the Sea Course, in a match when David and I as partners would play against Harry Bentley and another Professional, and we had some cracking games, for though Harry was getting on in years he was still a tidy golfer who could cope with the windswept links, having spent much of his younger life on the Lancashire and Cheshire coast courses.

We would always finish with a huge and well-lubricated luncheon at Le Manoir, having of course first been assisted through the 9th by Charles, and then again at the 13th green, Harry used to sign the cheque first, for this was always a special day and worth a thousand pounds of anyone's money.

After lunch we would say our farewells, David and I would get into the open Rolls and he would whisk me off to the airport.

101

I made that annual visit for eleven years, then, for some reason that now escapes me, I decided not to. It was on the occasion of our annual match, this time played as a threesome: Harry Bentley, David and Jack Ramsden, who was the Professional at Porter's Park Golf Club until his recent retirement and who had made up the four in past years.

The game over, including the pit-stops, then the luncheon enjoyed, with a toast to absent friends, the trio split up. David left the driveway in his normal manner, this time with an empty passenger seat. Somehow, for he could never remember, David was hit by another vehicle with such force that the Rolls was flung across the roadway into a concrete telegraph pole which, once the accident was over, was found to be still standing, but right where the passenger seat used to be.

Dear David's egg-throwing days came to an end quietly many years later at his home, which overlooks the new course at Sotogrande, on the south coast of Spain – a large white building directly opposite the front of the clubhouse, and for many years the only house on that property. Fortunately I was able to enjoy just one more game of golf with him there the year before he died. Every now and then, when no one is looking, I throw an egg in his memory. It always breaks.

22

———————•———————

ASHRIDGE -
SECRETARY AND GUESTS

Arriving at Ashridge Golf Club from Dunham Forest was like coming to another planet; this was a stronghold of the old school, where the Professional's Shop was expected to be closed by 7 p.m. along with the Clubhouse – unlike the past twelve years of my life, where Ann prepared supper for half an hour after dark, put the tray on my lap and went to bed. Then the main midweek shopwork was just begun after members' businesses shut down for the day.

When I enquired how Ashridge would feel if I chose to trim my tuition to just a few hours a day, the Committee looked at each other in a slightly embarrassed surprise: my predecessors hadn't given that many lessons in a week.

It was mid-winter when I arrived, and the only members who played mid-week were the ladies and a few elderly gentlemen who settled down after lunch to glasses of Kummel in large leather arm-chairs that surrounded a blazing open fire.

This was golf as it used to be – and why not? With only a shilling a year to pay for rent and a full membership with a long waiting list, why rush about?

Although a high percentage of members were getting on in years, there were, of course, plenty of active ones to make the weekends very busy. This was a happy and extremely successful golf club with all of the right traditions. The members enjoyed a good sense of humour and used to laugh when I described them at dinners as a club where if you were under the age of fifty-five you were a cadet member, and how I had found, upon my arrival, a trolley shed that had a hundred trolleys and a gun carriage in it.

It was run in those days by a Secretary by the name of Frank Sanders, and he ruled with a rod of iron; staff, guests and members

103

were all disciplined accordingly. I have always found that the best clubs are run this way, assuming, that is, that the rod is wielded fairly. A high degree of discipline makes a golf club function, for with several hundred members, most of whom consider themselves experts on greens, catering and administration, a firm but fair hand is a great asset once one has earned respect.

There were times when, I have to admit, I wondered about some of the rulings. For example, the miserable winter's day Bernhard and Geoffrey Hunt, the two Ryder Cup brothers, turned up with two of their members from Hartsbourne. Other than mine there was not another car in the park, the other staff all being resident. Much to the disappointment of the Steward, who had envisaged another even earlier closing, the four had signed in, made their way to the 1st tee and driven off.

The wind was sweeping snow across the bleak fairways, and was beginning to cover the grass; it was an awful January day.

Our Secretary, who had just finished a good tuck-in (the food at Ashridge has always been excellent), followed by his daily tot, had just arrived in the lounge in time to see the valiant four set off down the 1st hole.

Out onto the terrace he strode.

'Hunt!' he bellowed.

The group froze. 'Hunt! Can't you read? Fourballs from the 10th only. Pick up your balls and start from the proper place!'

With that he returned to his coffee and Kummel and fireplace.

I had observed this from the shelter of my shop doorway and thought there might be a reaction, especially from one of the amateurs, Jimmy Simpson, a scratch player who was known amongst other Jewish members as being fairly aggressive. They all bit their tongues and said nothing. A caddie was sent scampering off to bring back the balls whilst the players set off in the other direction towards the 10th tee.

Jimmy Simpson, through his aggressive attitude and immense strength (he was almost as broad as he was tall), had got to scratch in a very short time and was fanatical about the game. Rain, hail and, of course, snow, he played golf, much of it in the company of good professional players.

Years before, a friend had taken him to Hartsbourne Country Club and introduced him to Pat Keene, who was a well-known club Professional, though rather a shrewd businessman. The bug got Jimmy, who, at that time, was a very successful car dealer, so he made an appointment to buy equipment from Pat. Arriving in the Hartsbourne Professionals' Shop, Jimmy pulled from his pocket one of those wads of money that would choke the proverbial horse. 'I don't care what it costs,' he said, laying the massive bundle down on top of the counter, 'I want only the best!'

Pat Keene had a severe stammer, which tended to worsen as he got excited and now he was excited: this for him could be the sale of the century, a customer with so much money and no idea what he was buying. A golden opportunity to get rid of some dead stock if ever there was one. Soon Pat had a huge and hugely expensive leather bag filled with woods, irons, wedges and a putter. The pockets he filled with waterproofs, gloves and balls. Expensive leather headcovers were fitted to the clubs and the best veldtschoen shoes to Jimmy.

'Th-th-th-there you are, Sir.' Pat's excitement was almost over-coming him. 'Th-th-th-that'll be th-th-th-three hundred and fi-fi-fi-fifty p-p-p-pounds.' A vast sum in those days.

Jimmy picked up the wad and calmly counted out seventy of those large £5 notes, saying nothing until he completed. Then he turned to face Pat and, heaving his huge shoulders to their full width, he looked the beaming professional straight in the eyes: 'It is my intention to become not just a good golfer, but an extremely good golfer. When I do, if I find out that these are not the best clubs, then I shall bring them back to this shop and tie them around your XX!!XX neck!'

Pat hesitated, his hand frozen half-way to the money. Then he turned towards the racks of clubs and said, 'In th-th-th-that case, you'd better have this set.'

Jimmy left with the best and became a good player too.

23

———————•———————

HENRY COTTON

Henry Cotton's name was brought up many times, and many stories were still remembered and quoted by the older members. Henry had been brought to Ashridge from Belgium in the thirties by Lord Roseberry and other powerful businessmen in the City who had retreats in Hertfordshire. It had meant buying off the then Professional, whose name was Pook (no relation to Geoffrey who took over when I left), by purchasing for him a tobacconist's business on the south coast.

Henry enjoyed his peak whilst at Ashridge, where he purchased a large piece of land and built his lovely home, Shangri-La, which has now been converted into four luxury homes, and in the garden of which now stand about five others. He also had the benefit of the superb Professional's Shop, which, like the Clubhouse, had a glorious thatched roof until a young pyrotechnic set a match to the lot at the beginning of the War. This was replaced by the efforts of the artisan section at the end of the War, when all materials were so rationed that only a flat roof could be added. Sad to say, it is still there.

All golf Professionals owe a great deal to Henry, for, through him, professionals are today made welcome in clubhouses. Clubs found it difficult to refuse him entry with the style he enjoyed at Ashridge, golfing with aristocracy and driving about either in Bentleys or huge American cars, which he loved.

However, though some of the very old members used to tell me tales of the shop assistants in pin stripes, of balls only sold by the box, of members who purchased several sets every year, I admit to wondering why those who told me such tales still used hickories. Fortunately there were others who threw another light on the subject.

106

One day, when Henry had given his Assistants the day off to play in a Hertfordshire Winter Alliance Meeting, he offered to look after the shop so that they all might play. After a good breakfast (and Henry could eat) he rolled up at 10 a.m., opened the shop and prepared for business. By 4.30 p.m. Henry had not seen a living soul; by this time he had had enough and had started angrily banging closed the shutters, when there came a knock on the door.

'At last,' thought Henry, 'a customer.' He flung open the door enthusiastically and there stood a little lad, his palm outstretched with a ball in it.

'Would you like to buy a ball, mister?'

To Henry that was the final straw; he pushed the little lad aside, pulled closed the door, turned the key, and jumped into the Bentley which he had conveniently parked by the shop doorway in order to save him walking to the car park, and slammed it into reverse.

Unfortunately our young salesman had laid his new bike on the driveway behind the car. Half an hour, and many tears, not all the little lad's, later, Henry had taken him to Berkhamsted and bought him a new bicycle.

In 1939 Henry won the Open Championship at Muirfield and two of his Assistants from Ashridge finished in the top group of players. One of them, Bill Laidlaw, a marvellous young player who was unfortunately killed in a bomber over Germany, was an extremely long hitter. One afternoon whilst playing the tricky par-4 12th, a hole measuring 396 yards with an awkward gully across the front of the green, the youngster smashed a drive all the way to the green. When they completed the round, his partners couldn't wait to tell Henry of this feat. Henry never liked to be outdone and, never having got close to that green himself, wouldn't believe it, so out they all went, back to the tee, from where Bill Laidlaw drove the green again. I don't believe it has ever been reached since.

24

ASHRIDGE –
FRONT RUNNER

Under the guidance of Frank Sanders, Ashridge was a front runner. He started the well known Ashridge Pro-Am, which was one of the very first of the large Pro-Ams which are so common today. It used to attract as many as seventy-two partnerships annually.

Ashridge was also one of the first, if not the very first, to enter into the society golf market that has become the livelihood of so many clubs. By the time I arrived there in 1965, we were attracting an average of fifty to sixty players each mid-week day of the season.

Cleverly, he considered food should be a loss leader, so by providing a standard of mass catering that was unequalled at a low price, he ensured that more people visited the Club, the profit coming from the course in the form of green fees and from the bar.

Through him, Ashridge was the first to introduce the bain-marie to golf club dining-rooms, so large numbers could serve themselves and save on wage bills. I recall clubs such as the Berkshire and Royal Wimbledon coming to study this formula prior to installing similar themselves.

The golfing world was changing dramatically and clubs could no longer survive on the members' subscriptions; instead they had to attract income in order to maintain standards, and people with business minds were needed to run them. Frank Sanders had reached that conclusion and had shown the way.

25

---•---

HAVE CLUBS, WILL TRAVEL

Portugal and Spain

Another important change was taking place in golf: one which, in my opinion, has changed the entire way of life of countries such as Spain and Portugal. There can be no doubt that the influx of first British golfers and later those of other European countries to southern Spain in the very late sixties and early seventies has contributed to it enjoying the prosperity we see today.

A small group of young travel agents came to a PGA seminar and described the advantages of taking groups of members to those countries. They would offer deals which included the advantage of earning a free trip for the Club Professional as well as the opportunity to give a few lessons in warm sunshine instead of on frozen practice grounds.

In Portugal there was Estoril, Villamoura, and Vale de Lobo, and not much more. In Spain the Costa del Sol had Malaga, Rio Real, Guadalamina and Soto Grande Old.

Of the newer breed, Neuva Andalucia, now called Las Brisas, was the first built. It is hard to believe when I visit my apartment on the Aloha estate that in the seventies between the Andalucia Plaza Hotel and the Andalucia Clubhouse about four kilometres away there was hardly another building. Now there is hardly a metre of land without a property on it, and there are three golf courses all full to the brim. Peurto Banus didn't even exist; and, whatever people say of it, I don't think there will ever be such an exciting or successful experiment again.

I'm happy to say I was amongst the first to take a group from Ashridge to the south of Portugal, one of whom was an old colonial who thought that anyone living south of Brighton was categorized as a Wog.

The four of us had arrived very late at Faro airport, and after a long taxi ride we reached the hotel, where we split into two twin rooms; I was sharing with Charlesworth. Next morning three of us sat down to breakfast in a very pleasant dining-room, served by a charming Portuguese wearing an immaculate white jacket and bow tie. Charlesworth was, as ever, late. There is always one who is always late.

At last, when we had almost finished an excellent breakfast, Charlesworth arrived and sat by me. He then completely embarrassed the rest by snapping his fingers for the waiter, who, as a result of good training, showed no offence but approached graciously.

'Charlesworth,' whispered one of our foursome, 'I don't think you should do that.'

'Why not?' blurted Charlesworth, not even attempting to lower his voice. 'I know how to treat these Wogs, had to deal with them in the desert. They know their place!'

Our waiter was now by the table, order pad at the ready: 'Your order, Señor?'

'I'll have *dos* eggs, *dos* minutos each,' smiled Charlesworth, not even looking at the waiter.

The waiter didn't bat an eyelid, but turned and went into the kitchen. Our fourth member of the group spoke up: 'Surely Charlesworth, a two-minute egg won't be cooked?'

'You don't understand these countries,' Charlesworth informed him. 'They burn everything. Ask for two minutes and you get four. That's how I like my eggs.'

About two minutes later our waiter returned, the two eggs positioned on egg-cups set on a china plate; he placed them before Charlesworth: 'I hope Señor, they are to your liking.'

Now, some tap eggs with a spoon, others (and I admit to being one), chop the top off clean with a knife. Charlesworth was a chopper; he swung the heavy Portuguese blade; we all waited. The top of the egg flew past me and hit the wall. From the egg its contents flowed freely down the side of the egg-cup into the plate.

Charlesworth, now looking slightly more done than the egg but not looking up, being English to the end, murmured just one word: 'Perfect!'

Our waiter leaned over, his face a mask: 'Perhaps Señor would like *dos* plastic straws?'

The following morning a slightly subdued Charlesworth announced that he wasn't coming to breakfast; instead he had completed one

110

of those room service lists and hung it on the door knob. He went into the bathroom.

As I left to join the others, I was passed on the footpath, by no fewer than five maids who, each carrying a tray, entered our room. I decided to ignore this, carried on and joined the others.

Charlesworth was very silent when I returned, and was surrounded by trays of uneaten breakfasts, all of them different. It was then he explained what had happened.

The breakfast menu contained six breakfasts, a box provided opposite each so you could tick that which you required.

In true blue fashion Charlesworth had ticked the five he didn't want, and got all of them!

Florida

Travelling golf parties were not limited to Europe. America was beckoning and off we went in a Boeing 707 of an airline best not mentioned: Andrew Marchant, my solicitor and friend (an unusual combination) and Ken Swayne, an ex-policeman and self-made man and one of the salt of the earth.

Let no one tell you how difficult it is to get through the customs coming into Britain. It took our party over two hours to clear their hall at West Palm Beach airport whilst every item of baggage and more than a hundred golf bags were searched. That apart, no one should miss a golfing holiday in Florida, where the organization and service at golf clubs are superb.

We stayed on the third floor of an hotel that rose out of the waters of the St Lucie river, from which at evening-time huge fish would leap several feet in the air, a great temptation to Andrew, who loved a bit of fishing. So when the 'free day' came and Ken and I hired a Chevrolet and headed off up the Florida turnpike to Disneyworld, Andrew hired a cruiser and a captain and took to the water.

It was fairly late when Ken and I returned from our excursion and made for the room we were sharing, to shower and change for dinner. First into the bathroom, Ken threw open the shower curtains then leapt from the room in horror. In the bath Andrew had placed the biggest, ugliest fish, which was swimming back and forth – or should I say, swimming forth and reversing back, it being too big to turn around? Andrew had kept the monster alive up three flights of stairs, assisted by the cruiser captain and a pail of water, having left

111

it head-down in the care of his colleague whilst he filled our bath. Hearing Ken's roar from the next apartment, he joined us so that he might thoroughly enjoy his joke.

The problem came once the hilarity had died down, of how we would get the poor fish back to the river, for it was a species that no one eats. Neither Ken nor I wished to help carry it downstairs; we were both terrified of it, it being over two feet in length, covered in spikes and absolutely full of teeth, and Andrew wasn't strong enough to carry it on his own down the three flights to the water.

There was only one solution, since apart from the moonlight, it was dark outside. This was for Andrew to get the fish as far as the terrace of our room and drop it the forty or fifty feet into the water, which fortunately was fairly deep at that point.

Covering it in a towel to protect his clothing and to get a grip of this twenty pounder, Andrew headed for the glass doors. At first the fish was quiet; we thought it must be in shock; then, as Ken and I held back the curtains and Andrew passed through between us, our fish sprang to life – perhaps it smelled the river. Andrew struggled to keep control as he lurched forward, but his 'catch' was gone, all he had left was a wet towel.

The fish had landed on the parapet of our sun terrace, where, for a moment, it hesitated; then it disappeared over the edge.

'All's well,' we thought, for below was the river. We rushed forward, hoping to see the splash. Unfortunately the building was not quite vertical, each of the three levels below protruding just a little beyond the other.

On the floor below a party of newly arrived Americans from New York were enjoying a typical 'in-the-room' pre-dinner cocktail party with their tour leader, when our fish landed amongst the dry Martinis and Pretzels, scattering drinks and drinkers.

'God damn its' and 'Jeesus's' as well as other expletives rent the air; then, presumably the tour leader: 'Didn't I tell you guys? Didn't I promise you? You guys have never seen fish jump this high before?!'

'Hell,' claimed another, 'that's got to be a thirty-foot leap!'

We stood silently above, looking down until two of their number, obviously experienced fishermen, heaved the wriggling fish on its way to the river. Then we tiptoed back from the edge and went off to dinner.

Next morning we observed our American friends, armed with cameras, standing by the river bank taking photographs of their terrace to record this incredible feat. They certainly took a great fisherman's tale back to New York. We never did enlighten them.

Ours was a fairly mixed group from several European countries, many, like me, sampling their first American Pro-Am; but unfortunately we were plagued by a group of Anglo-Welshmen who, for some reason, found nothing to their pleasing. Apart from playing rather poorly, their misery was brought to a head on the Saturday when the news reached us that Wales' 'best ever' rugby team had just been annihilated by England. They missed the prizegiving dinner and instead went off to Miami to get drunk.

Next day the rest of us made our way by coach to the airport, anticipating our Welshmen would travel directly there and be waiting for us. They were not. Our tour leader, for whom this was his first overseas venture, had no wish to leave three clients behind. After some time the Americans quite rightly grew fed up and said we would have to load our own plane, which was parked some way off. The coaches were driven out to the hard standing, where, with the help of a few baggage men, we all unloaded them and packed the aircraft ourselves.

Eventually, when the plane was filled and another hour had passed, our Welshmen turned up. They did not receive the friendliest of welcomes, for the frustrated American officials had insisted the passengers all board and be seated and the aircraft be made ready to fly. The outside temperature was in the nineties, inside the plane even hotter, and we were stuck there like sardines.

Our Welshmen were not finished, and yet another argument was taking place on the steps up to the front door. Now the airport police were there. One of our Welshmen, still alcoholed and bitter about his team's defeat, was now refusing to board. The American policeman wanted him off the steps; our poor distraught leader, who still wished to return all he had brought out, was at his wit's end. The other Welshmen had taken their seats to much abuse and were saying nothing.

After twenty minutes our idiot had been persuaded to the door but refused to step inside. The heat was awful and the passengers had taken all they could when, from the rear of the plane, up stood a tiny Asian golfer, a doctor, whom none of us had known until that day, for he had enjoyed his trip in an inconspicuous manner. Unlike the rest of us, who were wreathed in sweat and had stripped off as much as we dare, he was wearing his jacket, into which his right hand was tucked Napoleon fashion. He calmly walked the length of the plane to the front door. From his coat the tiny fellow withdrew his right hand; in it was a syringe, which he rammed, totally without ceremony, up the bottom of our noisy friend with such venom that its contents went home instantly. The Welshman dropped like a stone, falling inside the plane, assisted in that direction by a burly cop who was sick and tired of him and had no wish for him to fall outside. Our doctor put his right hand back inside his jacket and calmly made his way, to great applause, to the back of the plane.

Despite the protests of his Welsh partners, their friend was dumped unceremoniously into his seat, where he was tightly strapped.

The fact that the Welshman didn't wake up until we arrived back in England would suggest a fairly powerful drug, even more so when the trip wasn't one of those seven-hour hops across the ocean: instead, for one reason or another, it took sixteen hours. Because of the weight and the type of aircraft, we were forced to fly up the eastern seaboard of America and refuel in Gander, from where we would cross the Atlantic.

Half-way to Gander, when we were cruising at around thirty thousand feet, the plane dropped like a stone. I have no idea how high we were when it broke its fall, but car headlights on the highway were very close. The plane completely depressurized, and all of those breathing masks hostesses show you prior to take off were bouncing amongst us in the darkness, for all the lights had gone out.

Many of our group were hysterical; experienced travellers like Tommy Horton joined hostesses and fitted the masks over fear-stricken faces. Eventually the panic was over and the pilot assured us everything was under control and the plane would be checked at Gander.

Hours later we were herded into a freezing and completely unstaffed airport hall and left from midnight to 3.00 a.m., when we reboarded. Those three hours proved fairly costly to Gander, for our party included many Scots, and the only thing separating us from the excellent display of whiskies behind the unmanned bar was a tiny padlock which offered little resistance. Gander airport's first 'self-service' bar had opened.

Once back on the plane, we found that, after many unsuccessful efforts to replace the oxygen masks, they were now sealed in with sticky tape. However, we were now past caring whether they'd be needed or not, so we took off.

We touched down in England about nine hours later. That was when our Welshman shot bolt upright in his seat, where he had sat unmoved and unconscious since Florida, and roared at the top of his voice, 'No I'm not getting on your damned plane!'

The best laugh of the week!

South Africa

Now our wings were spreading, and – thanks to Leslie Noble, husband of my first lady pupil at East Herts, who had taken up golf at the age of forty-nine and become a dear friend, accountant and adviser, and gone on to be Captain of East Herts and Brickenden Grange Club near Hertford – I was able to make my first trip to South Africa.

Leslie was Captain too of a fantastic London club, that of the Eccentrics, which for years had been the home of actors, entertainers, restaurateurs, gamblers and many others who felt they had an out-of-the-ordinary personality, and most had. Situated close to Piccadilly in Ryder Street, it was one of the best sporting men's clubs in the land, and I was appointed as its Honorary Golf Professional, a position previously held by Open Champion Dick Burton. Sadly, the club no longer exists, but its memories certainly do, and with many men.

Under the leadership of Leslie, a tour of South Africa was planned, and a group of thirty boarded a British Airways Jumbo, Leslie having previously privately arranged for forty bottles of champagne to be shipped on board. During the thirteen-hour flight, which we had commenced after a champagne farewell in Ryder Street, we consumed all forty bottles and arrived in Johannesburg to be greeted by members of that city's affiliated club, the New Club, who took us directly there for a champagne breakfast.

The entire three weeks were spent in an alcoholic haze: golfing during the days, and late-night parties at many welcoming golf clubs, which ran well into the morning. There is no hospitality anywhere to match that of the South Africans.

Advance news of our tour travelled the country, and wherever our coach stopped at an hotel there was a message from another golf club inviting us to join them. I recall on my return writing for *Golf Illustrated* of the fourteen great courses we had played on, my article appearing in the same issue as a colour supplement of Gary Player's choice of South Africa's best eighteen courses, which was a bit embarrassing as none of my list was included in his. But we had surely played the most hospitable.

Obviously in such a motley crew there was a good deal of humour and fooling around; and one of our number being a tiny, elderly, but extremely fit man, by the name of Sydney Sear, who always felt he was missing something, it was obvious that he was going to be set-up as the butt of humour, and he fell for it every time.

Immediately Sydney went anywhere different from us, stories were made up of fantastic things that had occurred when he was away. If we went to a party which he didn't attend, then next morning at breakfast we would all discuss the orgy that we had participated in.

'Orgy! Nobody told me there was going to be an orgy!'

Then he would listen to the exaggerated tales of what never took place and rage with anger that he hadn't been told.

When he went off to play at another club whilst we were accepting another invitation, which he did several times, for he knew of the best courses, he would listen to us recalling the fantastic late night braii at the club we visited, and of the dancing laid on.

'Dancing? No one told me there was a dance!'

Every time, Sydney heard exaggerations of the food, the champagne, and the women he had missed; we were all becoming experts by now at his expense, and he still fell, hook, line and sinker.

Right to the final day when we said our farewells at the airport to so many hosts and moved through customs to wait for boarding, the ribbing went on. We looked for various things upon which to spend those last few rands rather than be left with them.

At one end of Jan Smuts Airport there is a shop that sells huge boxes of dried flowers. They cost about £10 a box and not only will travel well but will last at home for ages – the ideal ready-packed gift to take home.

A dozen or so of us were in the shop and we all purchased a box. The shop girl was having her best day and was delighted with the Eccentrics, but not for long.

As we returned to the bar at the opposite end of the building, Sydney saw us coming, all with arms full of these gorgeous flowers.

'They're nice,' said Sydney, envious as ever.

Almost at once one of the group reacted: 'Didn't you get yours, Sydney?'

'Get my what?' Sydney's eyes stood out.

'Get your team flowers. It's been arranged; all of the team got flowers to take home to our wives.'

'No one told me.' Sydney was now bristling. 'I never got any.'

They were calling our flight number.

'Where did you get them?' Sydney was beside himself.

'Too late, we're boarding,' said Leslie.

'I've got time,' Sydney was not going to miss this one, as he had so often on the trip.

'They're all laid out for us in that shop at the end of the hall,' said Jimmy Amandini, a face so innocent anyone would believe him.

Sydney was off at a run; we saw him disappear into the shop, where the attractive young lady was happily straightening up her stall. To her complete amazement, in rushed this tiny, white-haired, red-faced shoplifter, who grabbed a box of dried flowers from under her very nose.

'What are you doing? Put them down at once!'

'They're mine!'

'No, they're not!' squealed the girl. A tug of war was now on.

'I'm in the Team! They're mine!'

The box broke open, out spilled the dried flowers. Two huge Afrikaans police officers heard the commotion and in they went, batons drawn. Seconds later they emerged with Sydney armlocked between them, his little legs hardly reaching the floor, the tattered box trailing flowers and stems, the evidence carried by the sergeant.

Sydney, swinging between his giant escort, was shouting his protest at deaf ears: 'It's been arranged. I'm in the Team!'

Fortunately the police saw the humorous side of the story when Leslie explained it. We paid for the damaged flowers and brought another box for Sydney: after all, he was a team member. Then we boarded.

California

Since those early days, I've been lucky enough to travel and enjoy golf in many parts of the world and, I'm pleased to say, often in more sophisticated circumstances than many of my early jaunts. Since joining Woburn, I have been encouraged by the Club to travel so that I might study golf clubs and golf courses, their design and construction, as well as the manner in which clubs, particularly in the United States, are managed. There is so much to be learned from America on the subject of providing the facilities and service that go hand in hand to make golf even more enjoyable. Whilst finance and the amount the golfer has available to spend has a great deal to do with what is provided, the intention should be, as in America and as it certainly is at Woburn, to provide the best possible.

118

Such an educational trip I made was to California, where there is the complete contrast of the fabulous links type of courses on the Pacific coast, to the more manufactured and manicured oases of the desert around Palm Springs, where the scenery and the clubhouse facilities are breathtaking.

As with most travellers to California, the idea is to start in San Francisco and work one's way south from there to Los Angeles and then east into the desert, so I started my golf as a guest at San Francisco Old, only minutes away from the Olympic Club, a venue of the US Open Championships.

The 'Old' is almost more English than many English Clubs, which it attempts to emulate, especially regarding the treatment of ladies, still seen here only occasionally. Golf had been arranged for my wife and me for 9 a.m., but owing to some roadworks and my poor navigation we arrived later than arranged.

We presented ourselves at the Professional's Shop around 9.30 a.m., where I was informed that, though we were welcome to play, my wife would have to be off the course by noon, for today was men's day and women were not allowed on the course then.

'We'll be all right,' I suggested. 'By the time the men tee off, we'll be well into the closing holes; they won't catch us. And if anyone does, Ann can stop playing.'

'You don't understand, sir, it's not that women can't play after twelve. They can't be seen on the premises.'

Ann walked, and I played on my own. With a caddie guiding us we reached the 18th tee by 11.55 a.m. where we were joined by a charming lady member who was also rushing to get in, so we finished on the stroke of twelve and dashed into the ladies' section of the Clubhouse and out of sight.

Once safely inside, and completely hidden from the view of the men, we, together with our new-found friend, were looked after in a marvellous fashion, for we had adhered to tradition, one of golf's greatest assets.

The Steward of the Club told me I should have been there the previous Wednesday, for they had had their special English Golf Day. This fascinated me, for there is a distinct English feel to the Club anyway, so I asked him to explain this special day.

'Oh, that's the day we do everything as you do in England. Nobody is allowed a caddie and we play two rounds in one day. After the morning round nobody is allowed to shower. They come straight into lunch, sweating. Then,' he laughed, 'they all have to queue up and get their own food and carry it to the table. Everyone has to drink claret at lunch, which is roast beef, and when it's finished, they all drink port. Then they go out again, still carrying their own clubs.'

I saw some similarities.

'When they finish, they get changed, again without showering, and finish the day drinking warm beer.'

'Isn't it funny what they think of us over here?

The Steward went on to tell us how, the previous Wednesday, one of the members was reported to be taking a shower, so a delegation from the Committee banged on the shower-room door: 'Showering isn't allowed, come out of there.'

'I'm not showering,' was the reply. 'I've played so badly I've just cut my wrists and I don't want to mess up the carpet!'

A feeble excuse.

The Monteray peninsula

One trip that golfers would all dearly love to make is that of the seventeen-mile drive, that glorious piece of coastline belonging to California where between Monteray and Carmel lies one of the finest selection of golf courses in the world, including Spyglass, Pebble Beach and many others, not least the daddy of them all, Cypress Point itself. All are famous in their own right and yet completely contrasting in styles.

Pebble Beach is what we in Britain would call a municipal, a public course, where the first tee sees a fourball, transported by two buggies, set off every eight minutes from around 7.30 a.m. until well after 3.30 p.m., whilst the clubhouse and the residential areas bulge at the seams and coachloads arrive to shop at the incredible Professional's Shop.

In contrast, and only minutes away, is Cypress Point, where the members enjoy their privileged exclusivity, where the Clubhouse seems more of an old English club and the Professional's Shop is even more primitive; yet if you are fortunate enough to get an invitation (and that is the only way you can play), then it is the golfing experience of a lifetime, which it certainly was for me.

I had, through various contacts, an invitation to play in a fourball partnered with a most charming elderly American who just wished to be called 'Boney'.

Whilst I enjoyed every minute of this piece of heaven, I could hardly wait to reach the famous 16th hole, of which I had seen so many pictures. Straight across the wild ocean the carry is about 220 yards, and average players play a no. 4 wood well over to the left, where the mainland curves on a safe route, from where a short iron shot is left to the green.

120

That was the advice Boney gave me when we finally reached the tee – rightly too I suppose, for the wind was into our faces and the Pacific breakers were towering spray higher than the level of the tee and the distant green; besides, we were already one down to our opponents.

'Boney,' I called him over and, putting on an act of bravado, the equivalent of Clint Eastwood, who lives in them thar parts: 'I didn't come 7,000 miles to play safe. I'm going for the green!'

Boney looked at me through steely eyes; surely, he thought, he's lost enough balls in one day. The caddie we were sharing – for, strangely enough, though they get paid about four times what a British one gets, there is a shortage at Cypress Point – leapt up from the bench. At last, after many years he was again caddying for someone who was going for it.

My mind went back to the many caddies in my life as this one listed those 'greats' he had caddied for who had accomplished this shot. I don't think that was helping me as I recalled the distance those quoted could hit it.

I teed up the ball; still he wasn't finished. 'What you gotta do is this, sir.' (They're always so damned courteous.) 'Address the ball and when the breaker reaches its peak, start your backswing and go for it!'

I decided on a couple of practice swings; the others looked on, Boney the most concerned. I felt my practice runs were not as smooth as normal, a bit quick; it must be nerves. The caddie must have felt the same: 'Forget those instructions – wait till the breaker's halfway down!'

I stuck with his first set of timings and managed from somewhere, prayer I think, to produce the best swing for many a year. I felt the clubface meet the new ball (I'd lost so many I had no old ones left) right in the sweet spot. I saw the ball take off, only just avoiding the last droplets of a huge wave. It was on its way to the gale.

We watched in stony silence. Would it carry? Would it beat the next breaker? Was the gale too strong?

The ball carried the rock-face with nine inches to spare and bounced forward towards the flag, stopping about twenty feet away. We all cheered.

It seems so childish now, but I was first to reach the green, not waiting for the others to play their seconds, and quickly putted up close; I didn't need to hole it just so long as I didn't 3-putt. It was the par I shall always remember.

As we stood on the green, Boney asked us all to turn and look back across the ocean. Away to the left was Monteray, to the right,

Carmel, and between them the finest golfing setting anywhere. He took of his cap, pressed it to his heart and said, 'Gentlemen, I want you to look at what you see here, count your blessings and thank God that you have been privileged to be here, and remember this moment.'

At first I think we all thought he was joking, for he plays there daily, but there were tears in his eyes and we knew he was not, so we all did as we were told, and I do.

Pebble Beach

The professionalism of Pebble Beach is a lesson to all who wish to run any commercial operation, not just golf.

Stupidly not realizing just how popular this golfing paradise has become, my wife and I arrived with a view to playing the course, Ann desperately keen to experience playing Pebble Beach, since she had yet to hit her first ball in America.

We approached the Professional's Shop where the course administration takes place. An Assistant Professional wearing an immaculate outfit, uniform with all of his colleagues, asked if he could help. I took out my PGA membership card and handed it over, for two reasons: first to introduce me, and secondly in the hope that it might do for me what the American counterpart does for those who present it at my Club, give me the complimentary game.

The Assistant studied it, then gave it back: 'I'm sorry, sir, this is a public course and we give no complimentary rounds. These are the charges.' He pointed at the board behind him.

It was 120 dollars each, plus another 50 dollars for a cart. Ann looked at me: 'We might never come here again, let's play.' My heart sank.

'You can't,' said the Assistant, 'we're full up!' My heart lifted.

'We are booked up,' he went on, 'a year in advance. Besides, there are thirty people up there,' he pointed at an upstairs cafeteria where faces peered from windows, 'who are waiting for a cancellation.'

Being a generous Scot, I tried to console my heartbroken wife, who had not had time to play San Francisco Old or permission to visit Cypress Point and now couldn't get on Pebble Beach, by offering to buy her a pair of socks or some similar item bearing the Pebble Beach logo.

We walked through the busy shop, which is about the size of the entire Woburn Clubhouse, looking at the most incredible selection of goodies. I didn't see any golf clubs; they're not interested in selling those.

A few minutes later the young Assistant who had turned us down rushed up and said apologetically, 'Mr Hay, sir, are you the Alex Hay who has written the book called *The Golf School*?'

'I am, but I'm surprised you know that, for it doesn't come out until next Christmas.'

'Yes, sir, it has, and we have fifty copies in our bookshop. Would you mind signing some?'

I could hardly believe this, for I hadn't yet seen the book, but I could hardly wait to sign copies in this, the greatest golf shop of all. The Assistant took us to the bookshop and there, amongst all the greats, was an entire row of my 'next' book. I started signing, I was going to enjoy this.

Someone signing his book is obviously something very special in America, and soon a queue had formed.

'Elmer quick, the guy's signing a book, get one before they have all gone.'

This was doing my ego the world of good.

'Who the hell is he?' Elmer brought me back to earth.

Within a short time all fifty copies were signed and sold, and as the last customer shook hands, the Assistant joined me, accompanied by his boss. 'Mr Hay, we want to thank you for doing that, sir. I believe we turned you down from playing today. Well, sir, I've rearranged things; you can play at 2.30 p.m. and with our compliments.'

My heart lifted.

'That makes your wife a single, that's 180 dollars.' My heart sank.

I must add that the price included the cart and we had a fabulous day's golf.

26

●

ALL AT SEA

Not all of the great surge in overseas golf travel relied upon the participants being flown to their destinations. Cruise lines saw the opportunity of carrying golfers who could be coached whilst at sea, then taken ashore at the various points of call, when they could play courses in exotic places.

With this in mind the Norwegian–American line decided to diversify into golf and contacted me at Ashridge with the view that Ann and I should travel on their flagship, the *Vistafjord*, to the Canary Islands. On board I would give tuition in a net, then once we had moored I could organize golf on those islands sporting a golf course.

In their enthusiasm to get into this new field they had omitted to consult with anyone who understood just how long a party of golfers took to complete a day's golf. Such detail was checked too late, and upon arrival at Southampton we met the ship's agent who, having checked through the ship's sailing schedules, often determined by tides, and found that it was impossible to provide times ashore, told us the golf programme had been cancelled, his reason being that many thousands of pounds of harbour fees would be charged if *Vistafjord* missed a tide and had to stay over. Since there hadn't been time to let me know of this revelation, it was hoped that we would accept the trip as a holiday at their expense.

Somewhere in a stormy Bay of Biscay I was summoned to the bridge from my habitual position, hanging over the ship's rail, by the Captain, a powerfully built Norwegian who happened to be a fanatical, though self-taught, golfer. When I asked where he played his golf, he took me outside to an area behind the bridge where a net was slung, before which was placed a coconut mat. This was where he had taught himself by means of reading a book and

124

hitting hundreds of balls whilst the passengers were at meals, which was about seven times a day. Occasionally when the ship docked, he would have a taxi take him to the nearest course, where he would rush to fit in nine holes. His very best score for half a round was 56.

I was becoming so bored by gentle walks around the ship as a means of gaining sufficient exercise to warrant the next meal that I was only too delighted to join him behind the bridge to hit balls and work with him on his swing. It was hard to believe that he could score so badly, for he had a glorious swing and could hit the ball 'miles', which he proved every now and then by thumping some balls in the other direction from the net, over the stern of the ship.

It was when I asked him to demonstrate a few pitch shots into the net so that I might check his short game that I realized the cause of his poor scoring. Every shot was played using the same extremely wide stance, with the vice-like grip of his huge hands placed at the top of the wedge, with each backswing as full as that of any drive. Then as he tried to slow down in order to play a very short shot, he invariably clobbered the mat before the ball, the clubhead bouncing from the coconut into the centre of the ball, which would drive forward, barely rising.

Despite the circumstances, I taught the Captain the principles of pitching, how the smallest shots are played from the narrowest stance, with the hands well down the shaft and gripping lightly, all three ingredients adding width, length and pressure respectively as the distance to the flag increased.

That evening, so that he might understand more clearly the difference between pitching and chipping, I illustrated a chart showing how, if he used an iron as though it were a putter, with little body movement, and hardly any wristwork, the ball would fly a given distance then run the rest of its journey, according to the club selected. The graph I drew gave the approximate ratio of flight to run for each club.

With each passing day it became obvious that passengers were being called to meals earlier and kept in the restaurants longer whilst the Captain worked uninterrupted on his short game. Those balls not hit into the net were lobbed towards the green canvas-covered lifeboats, which hung conveniently at ideal intervals and varied distances from the bridge and became substitutes for greens.

At the first port of call, where we were only scheduled for a short visit, the passengers crowding the rail, as they do when a cruise liner docks, witnessed below them a service door swing open from which, even before the ship stopped, jumped the Captain, clutching his clubs to him so as not to lose any into the harbour. A few strides took him to a waiting limousine, its engine running and door open, into which he disappeared. It roared off up the jetty.

That evening Ann and I were summoned to the Captain's table for a very special celebration dinner. The Captain had completed nine holes in 45, an improvement of eleven strokes on his best ever, and all due to his chart, which he had studied prior to each short shot.

More practice took place, but now we had to confine shots to the net, for passengers had begun to crowd the gangways for a better view. Such was the enthusiasm and so many the requests, it led to my offering teaching sessions, with the result that over forty passengers participated regularly, much to the satisfaction of the company, but not of the Captain, for others were using up his time and that of his coach. There was only one thing for it: he and I would escape at the next port, Gran Canaria, and get in a round. The necessary ship-to-shore call was made and the 'limo' arranged.

Fully dressed for golf, spikes and all, we waited at the 'Tradesman's Entrance' in what seemed to me to be the bowels of the ship, then a crewman held the door ajar. There was the limousine, door open, engine running. We were out, in and off in a flash and covered the ten miles to the south of the island, to the Maspalomas Golf Club, at great speed. We had a marvellous game, the Captain chipping and putting like a wizard. Nine holes were not enough so, as the sun shone from a crystal sky we ignored his normal stopping point at the 9th and carried on. His enjoyment came from his new-found success – out in 44 this time, another record – and mine from simply having my feet on the turf again.

Later, as we sat on the terrace drinking ice-cold beer, adding up his best ever score for the fifth time, the barman brought yet another round. He suggested we look towards the ocean, where, in a short time, the beautiful *Vistafjord*, flagship of Norway, which was visiting the island, would sail by.

'She doesn't sail until six o'clock,' the Captain assured our informed waiter.

'That's right, Señor, she sails in fifteen minutes.'

In our enthusiasm for golf we had lost all sense of time, our watches still zipped inside our golf bags. The beers were left, notes were flung on the table to more than settle the bill, much to the delight of our waiter, and we dashed to the car park, the Captain screaming at our driver, who had been sound asleep, for not warning us of the time.

What else the Captain said to the driver I know not, but we covered the ten miles in almost as many minutes and raced through the port gates, totally ignoring the guards, onto the jetty. There was the *Vistafjord*, ropes cast off, moving slowly along the pier, heading for the ocean.

As we hurtled along the cobbled jetty, we could see the first officer leaning over the wing of the bridge waving his arms, and pointing downwards. He had delayed the sailing until the last possible moment, when, under threat from the harbour master that either he go or pay for another night, he had sailed. Yet he was showing us that the passenger ladder was not yet raised but was being trailed along the dock; we could see the sparks flying as it bounced along.

Upon the Captain's orders our limousine screeched to a halt some yards ahead of the ladder, at which point we leapt out. The Captain and I caught the boat in the same manner latecomers used to catch my father's tram car, by running alongside gripping the rail and leaping aboard.

We played no more golf that trip, but confined our activities to the coconut mat, the net and the lifeboats.

27

•

MODELLING

Probably because of my secret ambitions to become involved with television, I was fascinated in seeing the work that goes into the filming of television and film advertisements and readily accepted the offer to participate in the only two I have ever been involved in, both coming during my stay at Ashridge.

A tobacco ad, most of which had been made in Jamaica, required some further golf scenes, and since the Ashridge trees, which were well known to the director, made the ideal background, it would be sensible to ask the local professional, me, to strike the golf shots.

'Don't worry about your face.' I remember feeling a bit hurt at that. (Maybe, though, on thinking about it, that is why the BBC have kept me 'out of vision' throughout my career, to the extent that once fairly recently, when introduced to speak at a gathering of Scottish motor traders, as I got to my feet a huge burly Scot got to his feet and burst out with, 'Surely yoor no Alex Hay!' I assured him I was, to which he replied, 'Well, yoor the biggest disappointment to Scotland. Yoo soond taller than that Peter Alliss, 'n yer jist a midget!')

The advertising director saw the hurt expression and hastily added, 'We'll only be seeing your feet and your clubhead hitting the ball.' I felt just a little better.

Comparing the fussing-about that goes on when making ads, and the time taken, even though one must understand the quality of perfection being demanded and paid for by the client, I am still amazed at the slick, unpanicked control of the likes of BBC's John Shrewsbury and Alastair Scott and their cameramen when everything happens without a moment's notice.

It took about six hours to get half a minute on tape, much of which was used up because of a cameraman who, to say the least, was blessed with an unfortunate disposition, got an insect in his ear and insisted after ten minutes of poking about that the creature was still in there. On the basis of my history of sound medical practice, my offer to disconnect a greens sprinkler and wash his earhole out with the hose was unacceptable, not only to him but, we were assured, to his union. This was a hospital job, and off he went to Hemel Hempstead, a distance of some five miles, where they syringed it out in a more professional manner. The fact that they recovered no remains left him fairly confident that it might still be there, and there would probably be legal action.

It certainly was not his day, for when he returned it was his task to film me (or should I say my clubhead) striking my ball. I teed up, and he set his camera on ground level about four feet from the ball.

'Which direction should I hit it?'

'Towards me,' he said indignantly. 'Why do you think I'm lying here?'

Apparently, and we only found out later as we assisted him to the clubhouse in a state of deep shock, his golfing knowledge only went as far as a putting green at a Butlin's holiday camp.

When my ball took off, even though I had carefully teed it up a touch higher than normal for a driver, it appeared in his lens as though it was coming straight up the camera, then its draught parted his hair as it screamed over him. He lay absolutely dormant for some time, his camera still whirring. Then it stopped and he started shaking. No more shots were hit that day; then, when they were, they were filmed from the side.

My next session was for a leather manufacturer whose advertisement would feature a combination of fashion and golf. A beautiful girl was to appear from a mist-covered forest dressed in a scarlet cloak; then she would twirl so that it billowed and flowed out and around her, and finally she would gather the beautiful garment to her body.

This scene was to be followed by me donning a matching scarlet leather golf jacket, which no one ever wears to play golf, teeing up my ball using my scarlet leather gloved left hand, which I would never do, for most golfers tee up using the ungloved hand, then striking a glorious drive down the fairway, another feature that doesn't happen all that often.

The whole advert was to be shot early in the morning on Wimbledon Common Golf Course, where coincidentally the traditional wearing of a red garment is compulsory, however, since we were filming about 6 a.m., it seemed unlikely that we would interfere with any members.

I arrived at the mobile dressing-room and was ushered inside, where I found to my pleasant surprise no fewer than three female models in various states of undress. Nobody seemed to mind the presence of one of the opposite sex, so when I was handed a pair of slacks and told to get into them right away, I did so. I remember wondering 'Why three girls?'; my script had only one twirler. Then I found out. One was the face, and she was being heavily made up. The other was the twirler, and she was pulling on exquisite tights. The third only possessed hands, that was all she had worth photographing, and her nails were being painted a vivid scarlet.

Out we all went into the chill morning air to commence shooting. After about two hours they had finally got the right amount of mist coming from a cannister blown by a fan, combined with the correct spin from 'the twirler'. 'The face' then stood in her place and the cape was fitted to her, and she smiled, and smiled, and smiled again. Finally it was the turn of the poor little lass who didn't have a great deal going for her, other that is, than a gorgeous pair of hands. She stood there, all four feet eleven inches of her, in the footprints of 'face', who had just been removed from the footprints of 'twirler' whilst they draped the cape over her shoulders. Then, when the camera moved within inches, these two graceful hands with their scarlet tallons appeared from beneath the folds and drew the cape tightly to her. Part one was at last safely 'in the can'.

By this time I was feeling slightly uncomfortable; I think I might have got into the 32-inch waisted slacks at that time of my career when I was sharing lunch with the Potter's Bar caddie-master, but a few comfortable years had gone by and these slacks were creasing me. However, because we were running out of the time allocated for filming by the Club Secretary, the director assured me they looked fine; besides, they were the perfect contrast to the jacket. We started filming.

The first part was fairly simple, except for the fact that I had a problem bending over. All I had to do was push a tee-peg into the turf within inches of the camera lens, then transfer the ball from the palm of the glove to my fingers and place it on the tee. It only took half a dozen attempts and it was done.

By now it was after 10 a.m., and already golfers were well out on the course. Fortunately we were located at the far end so we still had time. Nevertheless, I was happy when we moved into phase two, which was hitting the ball away; I wanted that over since we were using one of the members' teeing grounds for the shot.

They finally had me positioned exactly right for the sun, background and artificial light. I was poised, my stance taken, my clubhead against the ball; I was ready.

'Take one,' someone said.

'Roll it,' said another.

I hit it. I remember that, just as my clubhead caught the ball, the crutch of my trousers caught me. There were tears in my eyes, but in this business the show must go on; I held my perfect follow-through.

'There's something wrong,' said the director. How right he was.

'We'll do it again.' I moved up to tee another ball.

'DON'T MOVE!' he screamed. 'Don't leave the spot!' I froze. An assistant teed up the second ball on the same spot.

'Take two,' someone said.

'Roll it,' said another. I hit it again; the same thing happened.

'It's his trousers.' How right they were.

What I was feeling was not what they were seeing. Apparently the tightness of the fit caused my hip pocket to come apart as I followed through, and this wouldn't do.

'We'll sew up the pocket, that'll work.' I made to move towards the trailer.

'DON'T MOVE! Don't leave the spot, we'll do it here.'

He called for the seamstress.

I had no wish to complain, but I knew that the pretty young girl with her needle would never get inside my hip pocket. She saw that instantly.

'Undo them,' the director told me. 'Just pull them down a bit. she'll manage.'

There I was, my trousers pulled down, the pretty girl with one hand down the backside, sewing with the other, when the first members' fourball arrived: four grumpy old codgers who were obviously not playing too well and made no bones about informing us it was the Senior's medal and we should get off their course.

The Director explained his agreement with the Club and that we would all keep still whilst they played through.

'How can we play with him stood in the middle of the tee with his trousers down?'

The Director refused to allow me to move, so all four drove off standing just behind me. Sally, the seamstress, kept sewing. All four had varying degrees of mis-hits and the mutterings were getting louder; it was obvious that I had become the sole cause of their loss of form.

Finally, as the last of the veterans topped his shot, he could contain himself no longer. He came around Sally and me, red-faced, like a balloon. I was trying to look the other way and pretend this wasn't happening. He exploded:

'Bloody poofters like you shouldn't be allowed on a golf course!'

Then, as they headed off, another added, 'Just look at him, done up like a tart with her knickers down. Never hit a golf ball in his life!'

I didn't argue, but just watched them go. After they'd hit their thirds they came across my two drives, pristine golf balls sitting in the middle of the fairway. They looked around, obviously conferring as to where those might have come from. They looked in every direction, except back to the tee, then picked them up and went on.

Some months later I saw that ad on my television set. From the mist a beautiful young lady appeared wearing her red cape, she spun gracefully, the cape flowed, then she smiled at the camera, and her elegant hands emerged and gathered the cape to her. Fantastic, I thought, now it's me.

A red leather glove teed up the ball, then a red leather jacket turned and twisted. There was a crack of club and ball, and the jacket followed through. The screen showed nothing above the neck or beneath the waist, not even Sally's handiwork.

132

28

---●---

SUMMER SCHOOL

Whilst at Ashridge I was approached by John Bone, a master at Stowe School; he had the idea of opening a Summer School of Sport and felt that golf was ideal since the school sported an excellent nine-hole course, specially designed for children, as well as a huge expanse of playing fields suitable for group practice sessions. John himself had been a very good rugby player, and had many internationals as close friends who were happy to become tutors of that sport, so the two games were to link as the foundation for the Summer School. As the years have passed the School has blossomed, with hundreds of children from eleven- to sixteen-years of age participating in rugby, soccer, swimming, cricket, tennis and golf weeks. At one stage my golf school became so popular it extended to five weeks, with pupils arriving from many parts of Europe.

In order to persuade the Stowe authorities that sport was a viable way of using the school during the summer holidays, it was agreed that our first week should be a trial and could take place provided it was linked with the more classical and already accepted School of Music, where students came from all corners of the earth to study under the eyes of expert musicians, not the least famous of whom was James Galway, the man with the golden flute: James, a marvellously witty Irishman who, every night in the cellar bar into which everyone packed, would answer the barman's 'Last orders, please' with 'Twenty-three pints of Guinness.'

His pupils would gather around him, listening and learning, thriving on his criticisms of their efforts, and revelling in the slightest praise. Such is the dedication of the musician that every waking hour is spent in practice. This proved often to be a bit frustrating for the young golfers, as each musician requires an isolated, reasonably sound-proof area to practise. In the evening young homesick golfers

133

couldn't get into the telephones, the booth doors being jammed closed from inside, whilst musical chords emitted through the cracks in the ill-fitting doors.

Even the toilets were not spared: the rows of pupils' lavatories, which at Stowe have no locks, would find a would-be concert violinist, clarinettist or flautist comfortably seated, music hanging from the toilet-roll holder, hard at work.

Stowe is renowned for having many follies built around its grounds, several adjoining the golf course, and from these at all hours of the day and night music would float, affecting the pace of young golfers' swings according to whether it was Brahms or Tchaikovsky. Even the instructors' quarters were no boundary to these people. One afternoon I had to return to my own apartment, situated on the very top floor of a Victorian building. I could hear music as I climbed the stairs, and when I opened my door there was a musician, dressed in way-out clothes, sitting on the writing desk, his feet on my chair, oboeing. He took time to stop playing and tell me in an Australian accent that there was no room for any more. I told him in a distinct Scottish accent what he could do with his oboe and he left.

Even then the music didn't stop. In my bedroom was an Italian sitting on my bed strumming a classical guitar.

'Get out!' I roared. By comparison with golfers, and especially rugby players, these musicians are always so co-operative, but instead of leaving this one made for my toilet. 'Use the one downstairs!' I made to grab the handle, but the Italian beat me to it and pushed open the door. There sitting on the seat was a tiny Japanese girl, her music propped up in the handbasin, flauting away, her mind blind to the outside world.

Paul Way

To launch our first school and to convince the school governors of our seriousness, we had gone for what was called a School of Excellence, with the view of getting a high standard of young pupil and therefore producing good results and maximum publicity. So it was that I came across a thirteen-year-old abounding with talent. The young Paul Way was a natural hitter of the ball, and we took great care to help him develop his skill without clogging his mind with theory. One of his greatest assets then – and one which, in my opinion, he has lost in recent years – was his superb natural hand action.

134

I have watched Paul very closely over the past ten years, the first eight of which he travelled once a month to my teaching grounds, first at Ashridge then at Woburn, where we preserved that naturalness and watched him progress through his amateur successes and on into the professional ranks.

Paul, along with his school chum, Michael McLean, was being financed by a Lloyds underwriter who, as a result of his own hard work, was becoming extremely successful. Bernard Warren wanted nothing more than to help young British lads to have the equal opportunities of Americans, and was prepared to help them financially. He asked me to assist him, and I was happy to, especially since Paul, who in my eyes was winning material, would benefit. Contracts were signed to guarantee the youngsters unlimited golf, and Bernard's secretary, Bonnie, would look after their travel and hotel reservations.

Both lads did extremely well as amateurs, Paul becoming a Walker Cup Player, then too as Professionals, Mike, who was not a pupil of mine, taking the World Under-25 Championship. This he won in France, from where he proceeded to Las Brisas for the Spanish Open. Seve Ballesteros spotted him and came off the putting green to shake him by the hand, congratulating him warmly and reminding him of how short a time it was since Mike, as a boy, had played against him at Woburn and how well he had done since. Mike was delighted; he didn't think the world's greatest would remember that.

As for Paul, he won the Dutch Open at the age of nineteen, and there was a rush for the record books: was he now the youngest winner of the European Tour Event? He wasn't, by three months. Again it was Seve, and in the same Championship. He then went on to win the PGA Championship at Wentworth, in a play-off with Sandy Lyle.

About halfway into the five-year contract with Crawley Warren, Paul asked to be released: the McCormack stable, IMG, had spotted the outstanding talent and approached him. When Bernard asked me what we should do, my reply was brief: 'Sell him! Then use the proceeds to help some others.'

'Can McCormack do more for him than we can?' was all he then asked.

'Of course he can,' I replied. 'He can place Paul anywhere in the world, and contract him where we never can, for sums we would never dare ask.'

'Then in that case we'll let him go. We didn't come into this to make money, only to give opportunity, and since McCormack can progress him, we have accomplished our aim.'

135

Paul joined IMG the very next week, at no charge.

Later, at a luncheon, one of IMG's staff criticized the contract we had with Paul, claiming they could have driven a coach and horses through it and how they had laughed when they read it. That made me just a little angry, and I'm afraid my reply was a bit abrupt, considering the happy relationship I enjoy with IMG, when I informed him that our contract had been drawn up with only ever the lad's interest in mind. Had we been interested in ourselves, we would have had a XX!!XX like him to write it.

The teacher/pupil relationship Paul and I enjoyed drifted apart, not, as some thought, because of the contractual arrangements breaking up, but for other reasons. Whether or not Paul had any feelings of guilt, I don't know, but we were good friends and I would never have let such a thing hinder a real talent. After all I had gained a great deal of teacher recognition from his progress, and stood to gain even more in the future as his victories mounted.

What caused the rift was that he was all over the world, as I knew his new management would arrange, and I was busy with television. Often Paul would come into the commentary box after his round and ask me to come out and have a look at him, and, though I was often able to oblige it could be impossible when I had set stints to complete. I was also in a new position at Woburn, no longer the teaching Pro, but now the Managing Director of a booming club, and I couldn't put aside Board Meetings and such like to fit his demanding schedule.

There was elation when he was helping win the Ryder Cup at the Belfry; he kept coming up into the box after victories, would you believe, to ask if his swing looked OK on the monitor, after having just beaten some of the game's greatest. Then there was sadness as he slumped, and I felt for him; there was no joy in the fact I was no longer his coach.

When he arrived at Woburn for the Dunhill British Masters he asked me to spend some time with him, and I was delighted to do so, three hours to be precise and we nearly started a fairy-story.

When I saw the first few strikes I told him to put aside the advice he was receiving to see a psychiatrist: his fault was physical, and not mental. Where, I asked, was the beautiful Vardon grip of his boyhood? What was this right-hand palm-grip that was jamming his right arm movement, shortening his backswing, and closing the clubface into the impact? 'Give me your wedge and I'll show you.' He didn't want to give me the club. He was afraid to let me see the ballmarks on the club's face, for those awful trade-marks showed that hardly a ball had been centred for ages. All the marks were on the toe-end, proving how his right forearm was being forced to turn into the shot.

For an hour he hit shots, beautiful shots, whilst I stood with a club in my hand and cracked his knuckles every time I saw the right hand drop back.

What caused such a basic mistake to creep in? Probably the search for power; he had by pure hard work and exercise developed such massive forearm, wrist and hand strength that he had begun to overpower the club and deprive it of its own swingweight benefit.

When we met next morning, Day One, he assured me that his final practice round had been good, and we worked on the same theme for another hour. He completed the first round in par which, at that time, was good for him.

The next morning, Day Two, we went through the same routine, and we were having fun again, me like an old schoolmaster with his cane, poised ready to crack the knuckles of the erring student, and Paul reacting with a grip adjustment the second he saw my arm rise.

The fairy-story that nearly was, began. He started a run of birdies, and in the press tent I watched his progress, amidst a buzz of excitement. Going to 1 under, then 2 was pleasantly surprising to the golf writers, since he had barely made a cut in twelve months, but when it became 3, 4 and 5 under they sensed something special was happening out there.

Paul arrived on the 18th tee needing a birdie 4, the green of the par-5 hole well within his reach in two shots, for a round of 64 and to tie with the leader. There is out of bounds all the way along the left of the fairway from the tee to the green, where the writers were waiting and so was I.

Anywhere but left, I urged, which was exactly the thought in his mind. Unfortunately with that negative approach, and not trusting his resurrected grip, he led the clubhead through, its face open. The ball crashed deep into the trees on the right and then kicked even further in that direction onto a steep bank, amongst ferns.

The cool head needed for this situation, to play safely out and settle for a par 5 had gone. The long shot was attempted, the clubhead of the no. 3 iron catching in branches, the ball veering right and colliding yet again with a tree, sending it further right still, to a place where no one had ever been before.

Paul finished the hole about twenty minutes later in 10, for a round of 70. The writers had gone, and so too had his heart, for though he was safely through and would still earn a fair prize, what might have been a miraculous return to the top had received yet another setback.

Later that year, at Walton Heath, Paul played superbly and won the European Open Championship, even though he added a few more grey hairs to his No. 1 fan when he hooked that little wedge shot from a grassy hollow on the right of the green and left himself a horrendous putt back up the slope, and it was that right-hand grip that caused it.

Since that European Open he has had a lean time, but he will become good again, once some of the aggressive over-hitting is replaced with the natural grace only very occasionally found in thirteen-year olds.

29

---•---

WRITING AND DRAWING

A man who had kindly taken an interest in my career ever since he turned up at East Herts to report upon a Hertfordshire Winter Alliance Meeting held during my first days as professional there was that well-known writer and broadcaster Tom Scott, who was also editor of golf's oldest magazine, the *Golf Illustrated*. Tom was an honorary member of Ashridge, a position he shared with Henry Cotton until they were joined by my wife Ann and me when we left for Woburn, after more than twelve years service – An honour which I shall always cherish, as Tom did.

It was he who had nominated me for the post of Professional to Ashridge in 1964, but it was not until later he realized I had a reasonable, though very much self-taught, ability to draw. In 1973 he offered me a three-week trial of writing and illustrating my own teaching theories. *Golf Illustrated* was weekly until the mid-eighties, when it became fortnightly, and I have never once failed to send an article, even though I am convinced I am still on trial wages!

Actually producing a pen-and-ink drawing, the style of that time, made every Sunday evening a tough one for me. Tom felt that, even though I only had raw natural talent for drawing, his magazine had found the equal of the brilliant Ravielli of Ben Hogan book fame, which it certainly had not. I would arrive back from a full day at the Club and settle down to produce a drawing and sufficient script to fill two magazine pages.

I always completed the artwork first in case it went wrong, then I would change the script to suit the drawing. Nevertheless, it was a five-hour ordeal, and it had to be posted on Monday morning. Anyone who writes articles will confirm that you never get ahead, no matter how good your intentions.

It was because of my drawing that I had my one and only meeting with Henry Longhurst, which lasted about as long as one minute. I am sorry about that, for later, in 1977, when he became too ill to commentate and Peter Alliss took over BBC's senior role, I was fitted in at the bottom end. From the wonderful things Peter, who admired him so very much, tells me of him, there was so much to learn.

I was asked to illustrate a short book which was intended for children and called *How to Get Started in Golf* written by Henry Longhurst and the proceeds of which would be donated to the Golf Foundation. The publishers, Hodder & Stoughton, asked me to provide a dozen or so pen-and-ink chapter headings. They gave me Henry's original script to draw from.

I read and re-read it in the train from London to Berkhamsted; there were marvellous, funny little stories he had entered, then struck out by pen, some of which used to amuse us all during his commentaries. I was so pleased to do this work, I had completed all twelve sketches by the next day.

A few weeks later I was a guest at the first Bedfordshire Golf Union Dinner, at which Henry was the guest of honour. He spoke fluently and brilliantly, though he did appear to sway about a bit.

After the meal, as he stood, still swaying gently, amongst praising admirers, I approached him: 'Mr Longhurst, my name is Alex Hay, I have just completed the drawings for your children's book.'

Henry looked at me over those half-glasses perched on his rather bulbous and now slightly scarlet nose. He appeared to be thinking for a moment, then reached out his hand and gave me his empty glass: 'I'll have a double scotch!'

I got him a double scotch, returned it and handed it to him. He looked at me again, thinking deeply. 'Cheers!' was all he said.

———————●———————

For a period I became attached to an Aberdeen newspaper, for whom I provided a fairly long running strip: being able to draw and teach was becoming very advantageous. I even became involved with the *Medical News* in a similar series and I believe I can boast of being the only golf professional to give a cure for a slice between a cure for haemorrhoids and another for athlete's foot, all published on the same page.

One of my most pleasant tasks was when the publishers Michael Joseph contracted me to illustrate a marvellous little book for them. It was titled *Songs for Swinging Golfers* and was written by that extremely talented musician, Anthony Hopkins. He had written humorous golfing lyrics, to be sung to Christmas carol music, opposite which I provided suitable drawings.

The book was an instant success and was re-published on three occasions. I still have people writing asking where copies can be found. Many golf clubs were having sing-songs around the piano at Christmas time, photocopies of the words being distributed.

From the *Golf Illustrated* series my dear friend and long-time agent Donald Copeman introduced me to the publishers Robert Hale, who wanted me to write and illustrate my own book. They gave me May, June and July to complete it, my busiest months. Take it or leave it was the offer, naturally I took it (everyone wants to write his first book) and it took them almost two years to produce it. I learned a valuable lesson about publishers: they always want everything in three months.

I owe a great deal to *The Mechanics of Golf* which is enjoying yet another re-print as a paperback. The United States PGA School uses it often to explain the changes that took place in the golf swing during the middle part of this century. Because of it I was able to produce six more, including *The Golf School*, which got me on to Pebble Beach, and *The Handbook of Golf*, which is in several languages and became a bestseller in the series.

30

●

AFTER DINNER

Another activity in my life that was developing and which, in a sense, led to my involvement with BBC television, was that of speaking at dinners. A dear friend and fellow-Club Professional, and one of the best in the speaking business, John Stirling, persuaded me to have a go. It was a much easier way of earning a living than standing out on some icy, gale-swept teaching ground.

Obviously, to be any good one needs experience, and this is best gained the hard way, speaking where anyone will have you for little or no money, usually for charity, and where the audiences feel they are funnier than you and, unfortunately, often are.

Some evenings I would come home, bits of bread roll still sticking to my suit where they had struck, and Ann would sit up in bed, having heard me slam the doors and kick the dog, or anything else that got in my way, and ask me why I did it.

'After all,' she would rightly claim, 'you have a good job, and a teaching reputation. Do you really need to do this?'

'One night,' I replied, 'someone from the BBC Television will be there and he'll offer me a job.'

After about six years of exploiting my hobby, obviously assisted by my magazine work and my books, as well as my past association with Ashridge and my new position with Woburn, I was still being asked to 'sing for my supper'. Often, when I referred to a fee, there would be a stunned silence at the other end of the telephone.

'You'll get your dinner free,' was a regular form of payment offered.

One day I received a call inviting me to speak at a luncheon.

'Which golf club are you?' I enquired.

'It's not a golf lunch, it's a gymkhana.'

'I know nothing about horses!'

'Nor do I, mate, I'm a plumber. We sell lavatory fittings and we sponsor the nags jumping. We want someone to say a few words to our buyers in our marquee.'

'How much are you offering?' Knowing that every house has at least one lavatory, I knew they'd have a few bob to spare.

'It's a charity do! There's no money in it.'

That was when I declined.

'What a pity, David Coleman is coming, his daughter is riding, and he's a golfer. I thought you'd like to have met him.'

'I'll do it!' Was this the moment I was waiting for?

'There's no money,' he re-affirmed, but it no longer mattered.

I turned up on a miserable day, when rain battered on the canvas roof as customers milled amongst the brass fittings and T-joints. Then, after the paste sandwiches and sausage rolls and amidst the noise of toilets flushing, I was introduced as 'someone who speaks'.

Fifteen, fortunate for me, minutes later David Coleman came up to me and asked me the question I'd heard a thousand times in my dreams: 'Alex, why are you not doing this on television?'

I gripped David by the lapels and said, 'David, I've waited six bloody years to hear that!'

'You'll wait no longer,' said David, and he was as good as his word: I received a call the next day from Slim Wilkinson, Director of BBC's golf coverage and joined the team on trial at Birkdale during the 1978 PGA Championship. The following month I was invited to St Andrews for all four days of the Open, and have been with the team ever since.

It is the intention of the after-dinner speaker to amuse the gathering after they have enjoyed a good meal in convivial company, and hopefully with more than an adequate supply of wine, for they are generally more receptive then. As well as amusing, there is often amusement for the speaker who witnesses, in the words of Robbie Burns, 'the best laid schemes . . . Gang aft a–gley'.

So many clubs attempt to squeeze in too many speakers, and usually there is always one who goes on longer than planned. At one such club, recognized for its great golfing traditions, when we had listened rather longer than one would hope, I was eventually introduced and got to my feet.

Five minutes into my 'act' the kitchen doors opened, and in came an army of waitresses and started clearing up the debris from the tables. Cups, saucers, plates, glasses and bottles, everything that rattled.

The Club Captain leapt to his feet: 'Steward, get these people out of here!' The Steward appeared and ushered his ladies from the room. The Captain apologized profusely, begging me to continue with what is the best of my tales, which had come to a halt just before the punch-line was delivered. 'It won't happen again,' he promised. It did! Fifteen minutes later in they all came again. 'We've got a bus to catch, you'll have to wait!' So I sat down and we did.

I think the funniest evening took place at another extremely well-known club, on the south coast. The Club Captain, who was keen to put up a good show (most Captains are, and many do), had invited not one but two after-dinner speakers, my good friend Peter Alliss and me, and had not warned either of us.

Peter was not too pleased and was not only surprised to see me but equally so at the number of guests who turned up. Knowing the Club well he whispered to me, 'They haven't got a room in the building big enough for this lot, they'll never get them all in.'

He was right: there was not a single room big enough but there were two with a connecting doorway. The door which was at the end of the rooms, had been removed and the top table passed through the gap. Half the audience sat in one room and the rest in the other. The microphone, which would obviously be essential, was placed by the door-jamb, showing that the speaker would be positioned in the junction, from where he would be seen, Harry Worth-like, by both groups.

Whilst waiting to see how this would work, we were served with the Captain's choice of dinner. Half a duckling each for two hundred people, to be prepared by the poor stewardess on a gas cooker with three rings, one of which was 'on the blink'. As the first-served attempted to stick their forks into the duck à l'orange, penetration was possible, only as far as the point reached by the process of the defrosting. Then the first of the half-birds, shot from the plate to land on the floor with a resounding crack. Others followed, whilst from those that remained on their plates blood oozed.

Finally, after a harassing time for the unfortunate staff, for it was not their fault, it was time for the speeches. The engineer who had wired up the rooms had done so and tested the mike whilst the door was still attached and all had been well. Without the door, there was a different result: there came from our mike a screeching, reverberating whistle when anyone spoke – a fact we found out only when the Captain took his place, one foot and half of his body in each room.

After two attempts, which nearly deafened everyone, he switched the mike off and wisely announced in a very husky voice that he had developed a sore throat and would have to leave the speaking to the guests. With that he announced Peter, who was now smiling through cold teeth – an expression I knew well.

The Captain moved out, and Peter left his seat to take up prime viewing position, from where he delivered the briefest speech in his career: 'Since Alex Hay and I both tell the same stories there's not much point in you hearing the same speech twice. So I'd like to introduce my friend, Alex Hay.' Peter returned to his chair next to mine, sat down and wished me luck.

I recall standing there, looking at the dividing wall with its screwholes, and from each eye seeing half the audience. I unfortunately applied what I was unaware until that evening was my normal technique, turning my head from left to right, and right to left, a means of making the audience feel you are talking to all of them. I later found that each lot heard only one half of every story with only those where I was facing at the time, hearing the punch-line.

———————●———————

Many hosts have had their fun at my expense. Once in South Wales I was being welcomed to Llannelli by the Chairman of the local club, who claimed, in his melodious Welsh accent, that he had actually built his entire swing on my series in the *Golf Illustrated*, which he received with eager anticipation every Thursday.

Pointing towards me, he first flattered me by informing the audience that: 'Not only does Alex write the script, he draws the pictures, from which, by placing the magazine by the bathroom mirror, I have copied and shaped my swing!'

Even more flattery followed, as he described how, on a particular Thursday, when he was due to play with the Captain of Ashburnam and two English guests (pronounced Hinglish), he found on my page Gary Player illustrated in his famous 'K'-shaped address position. 'This,' the speaker had thought, having viewed himself in the mirror,

145

'is the final link in the chain of perfection that will surely bring my swing to its peak.'

On the 1st tee he met the guests, who drove off into bunkers and bushes, 'like the Hinglish do'. Then it was his turn. 'How could I fail with such a teacher?' he asked – more flattery.

Applying all he had learned, plus his new 'K'-shape, where the left shoulder is high whilst the right is low, the right knee kinking inwards, as does the right elbow too, 'Into the backswing I turned, like last week's subject, Arnold Palmer, my left wrist arching just as Bill Rogers does it. As I hit the ball, my left wrist supinated like Hogan, from the Christmas issue. Off went the ball like a bullet,' he stretched and deliberated his words, '250 yards, right down the middle.'

Looking down at me, smiling, his flattery continued: 'What a teacher, I owed it all to this Scot.' The crowd cheered in an anti-Hinglish manner, then he timed it perfectly, the sting: 'One of the Hinglishmen turned to the Captain and said, "I say, he plays bloody well for a cripple"!'

———————————————●———————————————

I have enjoyed the privilege of dining and speaking with members of the royal family, leading politicians, judges, actors, the best golfers in the world and many sports personalities, and, most difficult of all, I have shared the microphone with comedians like Jimmy Tarbuck, Frank Carson, Jerry Stevens, Bruce Forsyth, Dickie Henderson, Max Boyce and others, many of whom I am happy to call friends.

Soon after the Falklands War I was asked to travel to Hereford, the home of the SAS, and participate in a round of golf, followed by a dinner at which I would speak along with Max Boyce and Dickie Henderson; the proceeds we would raise would go to the families of those SAS men who had lost their lives.

Although I dearly wanted to attend, I had to take my family home to Woburn from Troon, where the BBC was televising the Open. How could I get to Hereford for the following morning?

'If you can get to Battersea by 9 a.m., you'll be met by "a man named Flynn", he'll get you to Hereford. This is top secret.'

I remember standing by the kerb at Battersea, my clubs on my shoulder, when a car pulled up beside me. Could this be 'a man named Flynn'? I was expecting someone wearing a bowler, with a carnation in his buttonhole and a copy of *The Times* under his arm. Instead out got Dickie Henderson, with his clubs. He looked at me. 'Is your name Flynn?'

At that moment a smoky, heavily camouflaged helicopter came in low across the Thames and landed only feet away. Out jumped a little guy wearing a tee-shirt, faded jeans and training shoes: 'My name's Flynn, get in!'

We were in and off in seconds, skimming the Thames as though avoiding radar or recognition. The machine, like Flynn, was not long back from the Falklands and it was certainly a basic model; nevertheless, it gave both of us food for our speech – especially when a team of parachutists leapt from it on to the golf course to present each of us with a named shield; the plan for the sky divers was to identify the player named on the trophy he carried and land at his feet. My man fell into a bunker.

The dinner was a wonderful affair. Dickie, the master of timing, and Max, as only Max can be, involving the audience. As for me, well I did my thing and enjoyed every minute. The result was that a large sum of money was earned by an evening that ended at 2.30 a.m.

31

JIMMY TARBUCK

Another very funny man with an insatiable appetite for golf is Jimmy Tarbuck. He plays a higher standard than many of his celebrated colleagues and travels everywhere to compete in the Pro-Am events that precede major tournaments, so helping to raise large sums for charity.

His first visit to Woburn was in fact the very first time television filming ever took place there. One of America's top players, Billy Casper, was making a series of instructional films and Jim and footballer Bobby Charlton were to be his guinea-pigs.

The trio stood on tee with Casper in the centre, his arms around the others' shoulders. He had just jetted in, but with true American professionalism he went smoothly into action as the cameras rolled.

'Hi, folks! I'm Billy Casper and I wanna' introduce you to a couple of very good friends of mine here at the beautiful WOBUCK Country Club. First Jimmy TARBURN.'

Jim's face never changed, not even a flicker. Casper went on: 'One of England's best-known entertainers. Welcome, Jimmy.'

Jim replied, 'I wanna' say, what a great thrill it is being here with you, Arnie.' Casper's reaction wasn't quite so calm.

Some years later, after I had described Jimmy's swing in a magazine article as 'being a bit on the short side, due to a lack of good shoulder turn' (which, though we are good friends, I don't think pleased him too much), he certainly took the opportunity of sweet revenge.

I had arrived a day early at Ferndown for the television coverage of the Hennessy International Tournament and was making my leisurely way from the car park to the clubhouse past the European Tour Office, where a bit of commotion was taking place. Apparently, although not involved in the actual tournament, Scotland's Brian Barnes had been sent an invitation to the Pro-Am which had never reached him and he was off fishing somewhere. Brian was due to tee off behind Sandy Lyle as last of the Scottish representatives, and just ahead of Nick Faldo, who was leading the English professionals.

Panic had set in, for Brian was to play with a VIP, Jack Hennessy, over from California specially for the event, and they now had no suitable partner for him. That was when I passed the window.

Here was the solution to the problem. Whether I could play or not didn't matter: I was Scottish and had a PGA card.

At first I refused point blank; I was at the end of a busy television run, as well as having been heavily involved at my club, and had not swung a club for two months. Besides, I had no clubs, no balls, nothing.

'We'll get you clubs, balls, a glove, a caddie, anything, but you must play.' Tony Gray, the tournament organizer, was very determined.

'No, I won't!' I was equally determined.

'We'll fill the boot of your car with Hennessy brandy.' I was weakening.

I was given the local Assistant's set of clubs and was in the locker room donning my new 'gear' when I made the mistake of telling Jimmy Tarbuck what was happening and how I was going to persuade the starter to permit me to hit off without an announcement, before anyone realized what was happening. Jimmy was due to play in the English squad just behind us; he wished me luck, apparently sympathetic to my situation.

The 1st tee was surrounded by several hundred spectators, so I disappeared behind the Clubhouse and, in the hope of loosening up stiff muscles, thrashed about at a few daisies with a driver that certainly didn't suit me. I then slipped quietly onto the tee.

Lyle had sent a boomer some 300 yards down the fairway and we were next off. The starter asked how I should be introduced, and despite his reluctance I managed to persuade him to allow me to hit off without announcement. I could actually go before Lyle played his second shot, for I wouldn't get within miles of him; the spectators wouldn't know until too late.

Having met my affable partner, Jack Hennessy, and explained my plan, which confused him totally since Tony Gray had told him of my great talent and how I had been brought at great cost to Ferndown especially to partner him, I then sneaked onto the teeing ground and pegged up my ball, completely unnoticed. Away down the fairway Lyle had reached his ball; this was it – by the time they heard crack, and hopefully there would be one, the worst would be over. I set the clubhead against the ball and took up my stance; the gallery's attention was on play taking place on a nearby green when it happened.

Tarbuck, knowing my plan, had sneaked through the mass by the back of the tee and got himself to the starter's microphone.

My backswing was just about to start when the loudspeakers boomed out: 'On the tee!' the accent was broad Scottish: he was impersonating my voice. 'Alex Hay, the Laird of Woburn; BBC Television and borrowed clubs!'

All eyes were on me now, there was no escape. I decided to swing.

'Watch now he turrrns his wee shou'ders.'

Everyone was laughing, even me. But it was now or never, so I started. I reached the top of the backswing.

'Seeee the FIRRRUM GRRRIP!' I stopped, was there no escape? Jim was now at his best, his face beaming; he was in charge and he had the mike. Eventually I had to hit it, so I walked up and swung without hesitating. It started off down the middle, then off it curved in a wild swinging slice to disappear deep into the forest. It was not over yet: 'Aye, he'll feel at hame in there!'

Fortunately things improved and we enjoyed a good day's golf; what's more Jack Hennessy and I have become very close friends as a result of the meeting, and my boot can carry a lot of Hennessy!

Next day when the programme started I was 'cued' in over my earphones by my director. The players were on the first tee waiting to play, so I informed the viewers that the ideal tee shot was down the half right of the fairway: 'This makes the second shot easier.'

Through my earphones I could hear the telephone ring; the director was answering it and laughing. 'Right, Jim, certainly I'll tell him.'

As I continued with my advice he told me, 'That was Tarbuck on the phone, he's asking how you know so much about the hole; you've never seen it!'

32

---•---

JACK HENNESSY

Because of the friendship with Jack Hennessy and his son Mark, Ann and I were invited to stay at their two homes in California, one in the desert at the Vintage Club in Palm Springs and the other in Hollywood.

The Vintage just has to be the ultimate in golfing luxury: not only is it exclusive to members; when they hold one of the major senior professional tournaments, called the Legends, they provide the prizemoney themselves and are the only spectators.

Once you enter the gates – and that is no easy matter, for you must gain clearance and be identified – you may then drive to your host's home, but you are accompanied there by another car containing security guards.

Playing golf with the Hennessys is also quite an experience. Jack's buggy, with a fringe on top, is fitted with a fridge and a speaker system. When I asked him why the speakers, I was told I'd find out. I did.

When Jack holed a putt on the 1st green, a remote control button was pressed and 'Irish Eyes are Smiling' blared out. When he's losing, then wins a hole, it's the 'William Tell Overture' that's switched on.

The homes on Vintage are soundly built, as Jack and his wife Shirlee found out to their cost on their first visit – a story told in Bob Hope's book *Confessions of a Hooker*. Their maid had gone for the weekend and the pair had gone inside a walk-in closet for their clubs, when the door slammed behind them.

They were unable to make anyone hear, and after a few hours a panic was beginning to grip. There was nothing else for it: Jack took the pitching wedge from his bag and hacked his way through the wall until he had a hole big enough for them to climb through – described by Bob as the 'best wedge shots he ever hit!'

Bob Hope too has a home on the Vintage and also stays in Hollywood, only a couple of blocks from the Hennessys, where we were taken to visit the great man on our last day in California. What a marvellous experience that was! A laugh a minute, and even though they were packing to fly off and do a Christmas television show in Hawaii, Bob still took time to show us his small golf course in the backyard. By playing from different tees to a few greens, he enjoys a variety of shots and has created a good test of golf, so he can play every day when he is at home.

He also presented us with a signed copy of the book which takes pride of place on my bookshelf.

Ann and I, returning home, were waiting in the queue at the departure desk in Los Angeles airport when the Hope entourage arrived in the building on their way to where their aircraft was waiting. As they passed, Bob spotted us, waved and called out, 'Hi, there's Ann and Alex. Thanks for the memory!' They were gone, leaving the whole queue wondering who these celebrities in the queue could be.

33

---•---

WOBURN AND PETER ALLISS

My very first feelings that Woburn would have a great and international future were being proved correct. It became a favourite place for television and hosted some of the 'Around with Alliss' interviews and the 'Men Versus the Ladies', where some of the best male and female professionals in the world played in filmed matches, as well as the Dunlop British Masters, which then became the Dunhill British Masters.

It would not be giving away any secrets to say that on very odd and extreme occasions, and in the 'Around with Alliss' series only when a particularly inexperienced player was being interviewed, the occasional spare shot was permitted. It was the guests' point of view that mattered rather than his golfing prowess. This proved necessary in the case of a young man, Andrew Barlow, who had received a new heart, and had claimed he was back golfing again.

Two three-hole games could be filmed in one day, so, whilst Peter was doing his thing on the Duke's course in the morning in the company of Lord Mathews, Alastair Scott, who was directing the show, asked me to have a look at Andrew and make sure he could actually play, as they only had his word for it: my brief, to make him good by the afternoon, but not to tire him out, for obvious reasons.

I have to admit to feeling extremely anxious about this pupil, especially when, after a poor shot – and there were plenty of those – he would immediately rage and grab for another ball. Even when I insisted that he have a minute or so between shots he would use up that time with ferocious practice swings, with the result he was working up a lather, and so was I, with worry.

At lunch when Peter had completed the morning session and asked me my opinion of his next 'customer', I advised him his task would not be easy. Andrew had an awful means of gripping the club in the palm of his right hand, so most of his shots were pulled low to the left or smothered altogether. The solution must be to persuade him to hold the club more in the fingers, which would hopefully stop the clubface from closing at impact.

I also advised Peter that Andrew must only use lofted clubs, suggesting a no. 3 wood for tee shots and the least lofted iron, a no. 5, having already made Andrew promise to stay away from the two clubs he had called his favourites, a very straight-faced driver and the no. 2 iron, a club so difficult to use that the average sets today hardly ever possess one. How he had them as favourites could only be from a sense of masochism; there certainly seemed to be a streak of this in his nature, for he appeared to wish to do everything the hard way, as though testing himself. He hadn't hit one decent shot with either during the work-out.

Each game in the series only covers three holes, so on the way to the first of the selected holes, a short one, Peter and I reminded Andrew of the clubs he should use, those he should avoid, and his new grip.

Peter was cued, and performed the introduction inviting viewers to meet this brave young man with the new heart.

'OK,' continued Peter, 'looks like a nice hole, probably about a no. 5 iron for you?'

'No,' replied Andrew, 'I think I'll use my favourite no. 2 iron.'

Peter smiled: 'Go on, then, I know you've been working on a new grip,' trying to help.

Andrew's first shot was sufficient for the cameraman never again to stand front left of the tee, the ball first diving between his legs then on into the gorse.

'Cut!'

Peter was instructed to do it again. Peter did, but only after suggesting that when asked what club he wanted, Andrew should take the no. 5 iron. Peter was not as yet experienced with Andrew's stubborn streak.

Introductions over, Peter suggested a no. 5 or no. 6 iron would probably be the club. Andrew didn't agree; he was adamant.

'The no. 2 is my special club for short holes. I'm very accurate with it.' Indeed he was, he put the second attempt within three inches of the first.

'Cut!'

Peter was still retaining his patience, although he was now applying that special smile with cold teeth that he reserves for special people.

154

Introduction over. 'Andrew, this is the club for you.' Peter stuck the club in his hand and was so relieved that, at last, Andrew didn't argue, but he forgot to remind him of the new grip I had spent two hours teaching him. The delicate finger-hold had reverted to a right-hand grab and, before Peter could offer further advice, the ball was on its way, swinging in a huge left-hand curve, to miss the green by about fifty yards.

Before Peter could suggest another, Alastair told him through his earpiece to go with it, 'Or we'll be here for the day'.

Peter had been provided with a very young junior member of the club to pull his trolley. It became Toby's duty to run forward after every mis-hit by Andrew, for it would be unacceptable to see spare balls on the fairway when the film was finally completed, and remove them.

The mis-hits were so regular that poor Toby was becoming exhausted. On Peter's advice, to save time and energy, Toby was instructed to pick them up then hide from the view of the cameras behind an adjacent tree.

It was dusk when the match finally got to within fifty yards or so of the 3rd and final hole, by which time it was fortunate that only Peter's ear was linked to Alastair in the production unit, where tempers were fraying.

Peter was informed that enough was enough, light was going, and there was only sufficient film left for a few minutes. There could be no more retakes: whatever happened was to be recorded.

'Right, Andrew,' said Peter. 'All square and one to go. A nice gentle 9 iron to the green.'

'No problem,' said our guest confidently. The swing was consistent with the rest of the day and the ball was struck from the shank of the club. Off it went, veering violently to the right of the huge fir tree that guarded the green.

Unfortunately Toby had not heard Alastair's instructions, and it was from his hiding place behind the fir, in an attempt to save himself further exercise, that he leapt upwards and outwards, left arm outstretched, to make a glorious catch of which any Test cricketer would have been proud. It was only equalled by the quality of his return, which pitched right by Peter's feet.

The show was completed with less than one minute of film left on the reel and no daylight at all.

Andrew, who finished all square, still claimed that had we let him use his driver and his no. 2 iron he'd have won easily. Perhaps his attitude was what drove him on, with his plans to live every day to the full, which he did, to his credit, until finally his time ran out.

155

34

WOBURN AND GREG NORMAN

Another series which proved popular and which was filmed over Woburn was, that of the 'Men versus the Women'. Players of the calibre of Johnny Miller, Jerry Pate, Bernhard Langer, and Greg Norman played against leading lady professionals, including Nancy Lopez, Sally Little, Jan Stephenson and Joanne Carner.

Once again Peter Alliss was the host, and the matches, though played in a sporting manner, were taken very seriously, particularly by the ladies. No spare shots in this series.

It was just as they were about to tee off on the Duchess course that we received a telephone call from Florida asking us to tell Greg Norman that his first child had been born. This was unfortunate for his opponents, for he was so elated that he sent drives the likes of which have never been seen before or since at Woburn.

His elation continued throughout the day and normal rules were waived when, between the filming of two matches, Greg celebrated with champagne during an extended lunch which we all enjoyed.

After the party, some four holes into the match, which was played over selected holes of the Duchess course, we reached the course's 14th hole. The gallery was made up of Woburn members and their friends and I was amongst them when the four players came past. Greg beckoned me over; he looked as though in pain.

'Alex,' the big Australian whispered to me, 'this is the first time I've played in one of these televised mixed matches, and I've got a problem. I'm absolutely desperate to have a fart!' Champagne has that effect on some.

I started laughing, so did he. That didn't help, his face became redder.

'It's not the women, I can get away from them, it's that girl with the microphone. I can't shake her!'

156

One of the very talented BBC assistants who provide the excellent sound effects of shots whilst keeping out of camera shot, is a young lady by the name of Penny Kift. Her instructions were to stick to Greg like glue, not only for the hit sounds but for any comments he frequently makes to his caddies and the galleries. She was carrying out her instructions with true dedication, her microphone, one of those grey furry things about three feet in length never far from the Australian. Everywhere Greg went, so did Penny and her mike.

I came up with the solution and explained it to Greg, who was now willing to try anything. I would walk down the opposite side of the fairway and pretend I'd found something of interest, and I'd call him over. There would be no need for the sound assistant to come; then, out of hearing he could let nature have its way.

As the girls were preparing to play their seconds and Bernhard Langer had gone forward, I waved: 'Come and see this, Greg.' Greg strode out towards me, his pained expression easing, but already our plan was failing. Penny was coming too. Greg started to run; our sound assistant is an extremely fit young lady and was sticking to her task. 'What could be so interesting over there?' the gallery must have been thinking; as Greg's stride lengthened, so too did our Penny's; there was no escape for the Australian.

Finally, nature called and was duly recorded for posterity!

———————————●———————————

Greg suffered yet another embarrassing moment at Woburn when, as holder of the Open Championship, which he won in great style at Turnberry, he lost £5.00 to me over nine holes. At least that's what I tell everyone. Oh, it is true that I took his money, and I still have it, but the circumstances tend to be glazed over for it was in fact the skill of Nigel Mansell that won us the money. He received a fiver as well, which he still has. After all, not many have taken money off the current Open Champion.

It was the week before Greg was defending his title and he was relaxing, or so he claimed, by watching his good friend Nigel practising for the British Grand Prix at Silverstone, only a few miles from Woburn's Duke's course, which is a favourite of Greg's. He won the Masters over it in 1981.

Nigel had just spun off in his final practice and had left the track in a rage; he had also found out that his engine had not been set up as well as that of his fellow-team-driver. The only way to unwind was on the golf course, so he and Greg and their clubs helicoptered into Woburn and I was invited to join them for nine holes. Greg would play our better ball-score for £5.00 each.

It is a strange experience playing golf with the finest player in the world which at that time he was, having led the field going into the final day of all four majors, though our Championship was the only victory he had collected. He was robbed in the US Masters when Larry Mize chipped in from about sixty yards to steal the play-off when Greg, safely on the green, appeared home and dry. Bob Tway had holed at the last bunker shot to steal the PGA Championship from him.

As a youngster I'd often thought how I'd relish this moment, teeing up against the Open Champion; I'd show him a thing or two. Now it was actually happening and even in friendly circumstances I could feel my hand shaking as I tried to put the ball on the tee.

I found myself going through my normal 1st tee routine of excuses announcing how I hadn't played for many weeks, and how rusty I'd be. Greg wasn't impressed.

Why is it that great players always do it? They stand so close to your ball when you are about to play; there were Greg's great white shoes literally inches from my ball. They don't even stop talking

158

when the game is for fun; he was chattering away throughout my preparations.

I offered a silent prayer then swung; my prayer was answered – right out of the centre of my club, what a cracker! 'That'll shake 'em!' One of my best ever.

Greg watched the ball in flight for a second or two.

'Nearly!' was all he said. Then he threw me another ball. 'Try another.'

Somehow, whilst Nigel unwound, I managed to halve the first three holes, then my partner found the correct 'gear' and birdied everything.

The next day Nigel added to his victory that of the British Grand Prix, which was something he was determined to do. I'm sure he felt he'd completed a famous double and the first gave him almost as much pleasure.

I know that I announced the result to most of the golfing world from Muirfield, taking care that Australian viewers had linked with the BBC coverage. I thought they'd like to know. Then Nigel also boasted of the famous victory when he appeared in the celebrity golf series later that year.

When members asked what impressed me most about the game, it was not those massive drives of Greg's, nor the wedge shots that spun back from their pitch marks; it was Nigel who impressed me, not so much his golf swing – for though he plays extremely well it would require a good deal of first-class tuition and probably more time than he has to spare if he was to become a top amateur. What makes him outstanding, and what you sense from him is the aura of cold, clear confidence. You can almost feel it; he'd certainly be one of my favourites in a crisis.

Greg is a man who possesses a charisma that endears him to many. He may be larger than life, but he possesses that marvellous quality of the human touch. There is never the slightest hesitation; even when the pressure is on, if something funny happens in the gallery, Greg's reaction is to have a good crack then get back to work.

The week he won the Open at Turnberry he was in unbelievable form, not only in his play but in his attitude. I was fortunate enough to arrive at Turnberry a couple of days early and meet Greg on the 1st tee. He played so well I walked both practice rounds with him. I have never seen the ball hit so far and so straight.

On the second day's practice, he was playing with Jack Nicklaus, who had given him one of those Cayman Islands balls to play a trial bunker shot, just to show how quickly they stop. It was Jack who had the Cayman ball manufactured to be used on a course built on a small area of ground on the Cayman Islands. It travels exactly half the distance of a normal ball from each club, so it was possible to play a shortened golf course and use the clubs one would on a championship lay-out.

Greg still had the ball in his hand as we made our way from the 4th green to the tee of the short 5th hole.

The huge gallery welcomed the players onto the tee with applause, now a tradition in the Open practice rounds. The hole was into the wind, and several who had gone through had required wooden clubs.

'Here's big Greg' – a Scot who'd been on the banking and, with his pals had been indulging in a healthy manner, the area littered with empty Tartan Bitter cans. 'Aye, he's worth watchin' – we'll walk a few wi' you Greg.' They began gathering up their belongings, bottles, brollies, waterproofs.

'Nothin' like watchin' a big hitter. You show 'em Greg. They've aw been usin' wids for a short hole.' Greg winked at his caddie, a likeable Californian by the name of Pete Bender:

'Gimme the driver, Pete.'

'Och away man, ye'll no need that,' claimed the fan.

Greg let fly with a full-blooded drive; the Cayman ball gives the same crack as a proper ball, and it rocketed from the tee, only to float to the ground about 140 yards from the tee.

'Gimme another.' Greg winked to Jack who tossed him another of the same species. This time Greg gave it everything he had; it landed about ten yards beyond the other.

'That was better,' said the Golden Bear.

The coats were being spread back on the bank.

'We'll wait for big Sandy, at least he kin hit it. That yin's gone.'

Greg played two more holes with the Cayman ball, totally confusing the spectators and stringing them along when they heard him betting with Pete that he could get up in three shots at a hole of less than 400 yards.

The joke was over, the balls went back into the bag and Greg back to work. I often wonder if our friends on the short 5th hole were believed when they told their friends that Norman needed a drive and a 5 iron to get up at a par 3.

160

35

---•---

WOBURN AND SEVE BALLESTEROS

Another show filmed at Woburn, excerpts of which were shown, completely to my surprise, on Independent Television, was a feature of 'A day in the life of Severiano Ballesteros' whom I consider to be the finest player of golf I have ever seen. We had some funny moments, particularly in getting Seve to the club.

I had been asked by the organizers of the Wrangler Jeans company to participate in a day on which they would entertain their clients to a demonstration by Seve to which I would add the vocals. Also a match was arranged where two sixteen-year-olds I was involved with, Mike McLean and Paul Way, would take on Seve over nine holes in an exhibition challenge match. It would also be my duty to get the three players to the course by mid-Monday morning. Not an easy task considering all three were competing in the Open at Muirfield and I was commentating; however, a private plane was chartered to bring us from Edinburgh Airport at 8.30 that morning.

Another reason I was charged with this duty was because of my friendship with Seve, which had begun in 1978, my first year with the BBC team. I had been asked by Kenneth Wolstenholme to attend an Anglo-American Sportsmen's boxing night at the Hilton and present the young Spanish golfer with their annual prize, given to the sports-man they consider makes a great sporting achievement. Although I had never met Seve, he certainly looked to be going places, and since we were both involved at Wentworth with the World Match Play Championship, I was happy to complete the task.

I learned that evening some of the now accepted facts about Seve: that if he doesn't want to do anything, he either doesn't or his facial expression leaves you with no uncertainty that he is not enjoying it. What's more, according to him, it always appears that nobody has

161

ever told him what is happening. I also found out, to my expense, that he has quite a sense of humour.

The night was foggy and there were massive traffic jams at Park Lane, so most were late. Seve was even later, he turned up eventually but wearing a blue lounge suit and a bright tie, when all others wore dinner jackets. He was making it abundantly clear to his manager who was with him, that he was less than pleased. Arguments sound even fiercer in Spanish. Fortunately one of the head waiters, who was Spanish, immediately left the reception area and returned with a bow tie, which our hero exchanged for his. We joined the fans in the huge room with its centrepiece a boxing ring. On an elevated dining area at the far end sat the VIP's including the still chuntering guest of honour, and me.

As we sat together, I attempted to get him into conversation, but he shrugged, obviously not in the mood: 'I no speaka de English.'

I remember thinking, this was going to be fun: the fifteen-minute golf orientated speech I was to make to a thousand lovers of boxing, and the only golfer in the room, for all I knew, couldn't speaka de English.

Fortunately my audience were good sports and though I'm sure they wanted me to stop talking and give the Spaniard his prize so they could get on with the boxing, they listened and, to my surprise, they laughed too.

However, the biggest surprise was still in store. I introduced them to Seve, a young man who had already won eleven tournaments and his first on American soil on his very first attempt. But before I gave the prize they should understand that he didn't speak English, although I was assured by his manager he would say a few words. Then I gave him his award, sat down and left him to it.

Seve took the mike with the assurance of a veteran and started his 'few words'. 'I don't know why my friend Alex is worried about me, I've been taking elocution lessons from Henry Cooper!' I'd been stuffed and the thousand were giving him a standing ovation.

———————————●———————————

The pick-up point for private aircraft at Edinburgh airport is by a small office building, well away from the main terminal. I arrived early and met the crew, who were already running the engines of a fairly small five-seater twin-engined plane. A limousine was bringing

Paul and Mike from their hotel and another was fetching Seve from Muirfield.

The pilot, assuming there would be ' a bit of luggage', suggested I put mine by the only baggage compartment, housed behind the seats and accessible by a flap near the tail. We would load it once the rest had arrived. Paul and Mike arrived next and we transferred their baggage to the side of the aircraft alongside mine. Already the area was looking slightly congested, since both lads had already acquired those large professional-sized golf bags covered in advertising, as well as suitcases and holdalls. Where was the other car?

The other car was late; the pilot, who was not a golfer, was looking distinctly concerned, not only because we were far behind schedule but because he had not realized how much luggage would be involved; his aircraft certainly hadn't been designed with golfers in mind. He stood scratching his head: 'Thank goodness there's only one more to come.' I agreed.

That was when the other limo screeched through the gate towards us: we could tell from the way it was sinking on its axles as it swung towards the plane that there was more than just Seve inside. Out they came, first the driver, then Seve, obviously in another rage, his brother Manuel, then Seve's manager. Whilst they shouted at each other over the engine noise, the perspiring driver unloaded onto the tarmac masses of suitcases plus three of those huge black stand-up golf bag containers that resemble something from the tomb of Tutankhamen.

The pilot, who was completing his check, had seen enough; he left his seat beside his co-pilot, exited the plane and entered the nearby building to phone his head office for instructions. Meanwhile the co-pilot kept the engines running, and above their pitch the argument grew even louder.

I had sensed what was coming and already had the two boys into two of the five seats and well forward, away from the door. It was obvious that all six of us were not getting into a five-seater aeroplane.

I tried to break up the row, for time was precious. From what I could make out 'nobody had told Seve that this day had ever been arranged'. I'd heard that one before, 'so he'd been wakened from his sleep and dragged to the car with no breakfast'.

It was only at this point that Seve noticed the size of our flying machine, and it took but a second for him to realize there were only three vacant seats, and that was the last straw. He was going nowhere without his brother, he'd had enough, his management were fired, he was storming up and down. His brother had to get to London, Seve had been promised a seat for him, otherwise he would have stayed in bed.

'I can fix that,' I claimed, hoping to defuse the situation. 'I can get him on the shuttle that leaves in five minutes.' The Manager looked delighted: it was working. 'Besides, Luton is where we're going, Manuel will be in Heathrow much quicker.'

There was a phone attached to the outer wall of the office, connected directly to the terminal. I asked for British Airways and got through immediately.

'I have Mr Ballesteros.' I didn't say which one. 'He needs to catch the shuttle.'

Most Edinburgh staff are golfers.

'I can have him with you in a few minutes.'

'For him, we'll hold the plane. Bring him over.'

We sent Manuel off in the limo.

The tiny cabin had become more like a lost property room; the manager and I had first got Seve into his seat and between us filled the aisle with all the cases that couldn't fit in the tail-end.

Then we pushed and dragged, shouting instructions to each other over the engine noise, the two huge bags inside their mummy cases, then somehow managed to squeeze into our seats. The manager's was near enough to the door for him to reach out and slam it shut, then lock it.

Surely we were off at last. The engines revved. 'Wait a minute, something's banging.' We all listened. Yes, there it was again, a definite thumping near the back. We all looked around – there, hammering at the door with his fist was our pilot: 'Excuse me, might I come in?'

Had I been him I would have packed it all in there and then, but I think all he wanted was to get back to Luton. The only way he could get to his seat was to climb on top of the mummy cases and slide himself forward, feet first, above our heads, then drop into his compartment, which he did, perspiring profusely.

After a pretty uncomfortable flight we landed at Luton airport, where a brass band was playing to welcome Seve. The officials of the airport stood waiting for us to emerge. We sat waiting for someone to open the door and extract the baggage so that we could get out.

After the band had played 'Viva España' three times, someone finally realized we had a problem. I recall thinking of the words of that song, 'I'm not waving, I'm drowning', as we waved and they waved back. We were finally released like sardines from a tin.

Seve was not having one of his best days, and when he finally got out, convinced that his back had 'gone' forever, a lovely young girl

164

wearing very little stepped up, kissed him on both cheeks and stuck a straw boater on his head, the traditional welcome from the town known as 'The Hatters' – Seve was not amused.

I have the straw boater in my study to this day, it was a memory that Seve had no wish to retain.

Some years later I felt very fortunate to be invited to a dinner party to which Seve had apparently accepted an invitation. I almost attended out of curiosity, just to see if he would actually turn up, knowing how he hates being with too many strangers. However, his brother and another Spanish friend had also been asked, so it was possible he would come.

When I arrived, I really was surprised at the amount of people in the room. I asked our hostess, a very attractive divorcee, how she'd persuaded Seve to come to such a large dinner party – apart, I hastened to add, from her personal charms. 'Oh,' she replied, 'I haven't told him yet. He thinks there are just half a dozen, but I thought my friends would like to meet him.'

Knowing Seve, I suggested to her that when he saw the numbers he might just develop a bad back.

It was cold that evening, and I was enjoying a glass of Scottish wine by a huge log fire when I heard the door bell. In came the Ballesteros brothers, with their friend, an older man whose eyes lit up when he saw the gathering of female company. Seve's eyes did the opposite: dark pools they became, the mouth dropped at the edges. I had seen that expression before.

Our vivacious hostess was by his side; the older friend was obviously already besotted by her and moved between them.

Seve looked around for a familiar face and spotted mine. He left the hostess with her new and amorous admirer and moved to join me by the fireplace.

'Alexi.' It must be the Spanish pronunciation – he always calls me that; Seve has difficulty with some words, though his English is a great deal better than he makes out, especially when he doesn't wish to hear. 'My back hees no so good.' He had backed up as close to the fireplace as he could and had pulled his shirt and sweater up to let even more heat get to his back. Our hostess temporarily escaped the advances of her new-found admirer and made her way through the crowded room to join us.

165

'Seve, let me get you a drink.'

'I no theenk I can stay. My back hees no so good.'

'Oh, please stay for dinner, we can start now. There's a table plan.'

Our hostess made off to the kitchen to hurry dinner, closely followed.

The table stretched the length of the room, and the plan found our hostess, quite naturally, at the head of the table, with Seve, quite naturally, on her immediate right. Seve's brother was at the opposite end, and the third member was next to me, about half-way along the room.

As we took our places, there was the normal chatter and clatter and scraping of chairs, but above it my neighbour was exchanging comments in Spanish with Seve which none of us understood – not until Seve informed our attractive divorcee that he wished to discuss the way the course was playing with his friend Alexi. He would exchange places with his friend, which he did.

Seve, his brother and his friend, who now had a permanent smile on his face, left immediately after the main course; Seve's back could wait no longer; nor I fear could our hostess, who had managed to eat her dinner only with great difficulty.

———————●———————

Being involved with superstars in company golf days has been a marvellous experience and I have enjoyed being with them at Woburn where frequent visits are made by many of the world's best. Normally I have the easy task of producing the dialogue whilst they have the much tougher task of performing the often incredibly difficult shots I suggest they demonstrate.

I have never had 'under my control' anyone so talented as Seve; and I will say this for my *amigo*, that once he has safely arrived at the venue and has met the guests he sells himself beautifully and, as though aware of the sums he is collecting per minute, really does his best to earn it. No one goes away who is not absolutely enthralled by him, though of course you must beware of that devilish sense of humour.

On the day we had flown down from Muirfield, he performed shots from the kneeling position; balls were hit from under his own outstretched leg, drivers were fading and hooking at the whim of the spectators. One asked him to demonstrate a low shot for headwinds.

166

Seve obliged and the 4-iron shot flew about twenty feet in the air, to great applause.

'You can do better than that!' I stated boldly, throwing down another ball, then treading it into the turf.

Seve eyed the plugged ball for a few seconds then walked across to me, took the mike and handed me the iron. The gallery thought this would be a treat; I did not and refused to be drawn in, for I wouldn't have got it out of the ground.

Then Seve claimed his revenge: 'Alexi he used to be a very good player. My Mamma used to tell me, she remembered him when she was a little girl. This is how he used to play.' He stepped to the wrong side of the ball, as though a left-hander, then, turning the club in his hands so that the clubhead reversed, its toe-end touching the ground, he proceeded to swing left-handed and smashed the ball from its half-buried lie, straight down the middle.

After an hour of good-humoured magic, he went off to the 1st tee, where he was to play the challenge match against Paul Way and Mike McLean, who had already practised over the nine selected holes. Seve would play his one score against their better score. He started off with five straight birdies and the match was over 5/4.

I have a feeling that the relationship that sprang up that day between him and the sixteen-year-old Way led him to requesting Paul as his partner in the 1983 Ryder Cup Match which, though we didn't win, sparked off the belief that we could; and we have since.

Communication between Seve and me was improving with every engagement, and the clinics were good fun. A good rapport is essential otherwise things don't always work out when you can't depend on the talented hitter understanding what you are talking about. Once, in Nassau, before a large gallery seated behind us in a grandstand, I was working with a good friend of mine, a well-known Irish professional who is renowned for his natural flair for golf and certainly not one of the ever-increasing theory brigade.

I informed the spectators that when a top professional plays a trick shot he is simply playing a mis-hit deliberately and to do so all he had to do was copy the positions that poor golfers engage when they play their mis-hits.

This boomed out over a massive loudspeaking system, and the gallery seemed impressed. My man looked confused. I carried on: 'For example, watch what happens when my colleague sets up as follows.' I then listed, virtually quoting the PGA training manual, the causes of a slice:

'The blade lies slightly open.' He turned the blade open.

'The left hand weakens back, so that only one knuckle is visible.'
His left hand eased off to the left.

'The ball is positioned well forward in the stance.' He shuffled to
the right, until the ball was opposite the toes of his left foot.

'The shoulder line is now turned away to the left of the target.'
His left side turned open.

'Because of this his backswing will be upright, and he will swing
across the ball from OUT-to-IN! Let's go!' I stepped back out of
the way.

He stood frozen to the spot. He was now whispering something
to me. I moved closer: 'What's wrong?' I whispered back.

'Will you switch that damn mike off!' he hissed. I switched it off.
'Now then,' he said, muscles tightening, 'which fooking direction do
you want it to go?!'

36

---•---

WOBURN AND GARY PLAYER

Another great player I became involved with in company days was Gary Player, a man whom you have just got to admire for his pure courage and determination. I had first met him in the mid-fifties when, as he and his travelling companion Trevor Wilkes on their first season in Britain were running out of funds, they had hitched a lift from St Andrews with Bill Shankland and had come to Potter's Bar.

He had barely won a penny and was on his way back to South Africa to re-build a swing that had been heavily criticized by the other professionals, some extremely harsh in their opinions. Perhaps that was the spur he needed, for the swing he returned with was one that took him past all of them and kept him at the top for decades.

Apart from his swing, he has his physical condition to thank. I have no doubt this was gained after remarks about his height; even now, though well into his fifties, he is fitter than many half his age.

He was playing in a tournament which was being televised by the 'other side', which I was watching, and was due to come to our home at close of play. He would stay with us for a couple of nights.

When the doorbell rang Ann looked out of the window and said, 'I think that's Gary Player out there.'

I was engrossed in the golf: 'Can't be, he's playing at Moor Park.'

'Well, there's a little fellow at the door dressed in black and carrying a bunch of bananas.'

Because of a fog delay Gary had been eliminated after only 9 holes, so had left early. He spent the time before dinner, in his vest and shorts, running up and down our staircase as part of his training schedule. Such is the strength in his fingers that when we attempted to run the bath in the room he had used I couldn't turn the taps on; we had to bring in a plumber to release them.

During Gary's visit to Woburn he was engaged by a company which shall be nameless, but who produce a make of safety glass, to play an exhibition round before guests and clients; then they could all meet over lunch, which would be followed by a speech by Gary and a special demonstration of their product.

Like many of the world's great players, especially those who have come up the hard way, Gary enjoys that marvellous ability to communicate, and during the morning he demonstrated and explained his mastery of the game.

After a good lunch Gary was introduced, and we found out his talents are not limited to the great outdoors, for he is a highly entertaining speaker.

It was whilst he was on his feet that those of us by the window noticed the activity taking place on the grass outside the dining-room. Three large frames, each holding a sheet of glass, were being set down upon a polythene sheet.

A little fellow in a white outfit, bearing the company name, who was obviously in charge, had emptied out a bag of practice balls. Then with meticulous care, he teed up three balls, each about ten yards short of the panes of glass.

Although we returned our attention to Gary, who was in full flow, there was a feeling of anticipation, for it was obvious that the balls were going to be hit at the sheets of glass. We had not long to wait: as soon as Gary finished, the Managing Director announced that we should all move outside, where Gary was going to give a special demonstration of their product.

We all shuffled out, most still carrying their liqueurs and brandies, puffing at expensive cigars, some of the perks of 'the company day'.

Gary had gone off to the locker room to prepare; whilst he was gone the Managing Director explained the merits of the contents of the three wooden frames. According to him, the first contained quarter-inch-thick British safety glass, The centre frame had half-inch US safety glass. As for the third, it contained nothing more than his company's standard glass

From our host's tone, we all knew now what was going to happen. Gary was about to drive the three balls at the targets, and from the Managing Director's obvious confidence, and the fact that sheets of polythene were pegged out only beneath the first and second frames, clearly only those two would suffer.

Gary duly appeared; he had changed into his black head-to-toe outfit, which he used to claim made him feel powerful, so there was to be no holding back.

Gary stepped over the practice bag, which lay on the grass, its contents spilled out as though in readiness should Gary need more shots; however, since the panes were about six feet square, the balls were there only to add effect to the spectacle.

The little man went through a few minutes of strenuous practice swinging, the clubhead fairly whistling through at the bottom of the swing, then he moved towards the first ball. The familiar Player mannerisms, the extended left arm, the push-in of the right knee as the right hand is added to the club, the 'K'-shape, then the famous forward press as the shaft gets pushed forward towards the target, combining with an even greater inward push with the right knee. The swing was in motion: the full turn, the tremendous change of the legwork which initiates his downswing. The crack of clubhead meeting ball, then almost instantly, even before the familiar high right-shoulder movement was through – a movement which Gary has fought much of his career – there came another crack, that of the ball hitting the quarter-inch British glass, which shattered into a thousand pieces. Those guests with their hands free applauded, the others either cheered, coughed or spluttered their approval.

Gary moved to the second ball; the practice swings appeared even more ferocious – surely even half-inch glass couldn't withstand such an aggressive hit. Perhaps it was because the ball was teed just a touch higher, or did Gary go at it just too ferociously, who knows?

One little Scotsman in the group – not me I hasten to add, and possibly because he had had a bit too much to drink – thought he knew why Gary had missed the window, and, as the ball flew from high up on the face of the club, soaring upwards and clearing the frame by inches, he gave his diagnosis to his drinking companion in the momentary silence of the stunned group: 'Ye see, if yer right shoulder comes up as quick as Gary's yer bound to balloon the ba'.' Everyone laughed. Everyone, that is, with the exception of Gary, who looked absolutely furious: he did not like missing the glass, and he hated being laughed at. With his driver, he reached back to the bagful of balls and hooked one towards him. Then, without waiting even to tee it up, or even for the laughter to subside, he launched into a vicious strike. Was it the tight lie, was it the hasty swing, or was it what the wee Scotsman said? Whatever it was, the ball came this time from the toe-end of the clubhead and was moving very fast, but to the right, to where the third frame stood, that containing our host's standard glass, which shattered into a million pieces.

Our Managing Director was not at all pleased and turned on the little man, not the one in black, but the one in the white outfit, who was reaping the fury of his boss. Finally he could take no more, picked up the third ball, which was still sitting patiently on its tee, handed it to his boss and claimed, 'He was supposed to hit it with this one!'

37

---•---

COMPANY DAYS

Not all company days are the luxury version. I was hired by a company to do a series of six, all over the country, where along with Peter Butler we were shared amongst 54 clients. To do this means that each pro plays with 27 guests, playing two holes with groups of three and dropping back through the field. Though you meet many pleasant people, it means that you are on the course for about seven hours, going off with the first lot and finishing with the last.

One such day was spent at Filton Golf Club, which, when the March wind blows up the Bristol Channel, must be one of the coldest places in England.

I had made my way to the 1st tee when the young Assistant Pro asked if he could carry my clubs; he was sure he would learn a lot. The lad wore only a slipover and I suggested he get a coat, but he declined, and since he had been brought up there he must know how cold it was.

It was when I said goodbye to my three partners on the 2nd green that the Assistant realized why I'd been concerned. He had imagined that going off first would mean a quick round. Some five hours later, when we were still well out on the course, he was shivering and blue with cold.

By the 16th green, when we had bade the penultimate lot goodbye, he was nearly numb and visibly shaking. We sheltered from the vicious wind behind a tree. 'Just one more lot,' I assured him; he looked well past caring. Minutes past, there was no sign of the final trio, Japanese top clients of the host group.

'Do you putt well?' I asked my caddie who looked all in.

'Not all that well.'

'C'mon,' I said, getting him an old ball from my bag. 'Borrow my putter and I'll challenge you whilst we wait. A pound a putt.'

I picked the first spot, one where I'd putted from earlier, and rolled a good putt to within inches.

He practised his stroke, his fingers barely capable of holding the putter. Then he holed it!

Ten minutes later he was £5.00 up.

'I think I'll have to go in, sir. I'm absolutely frozen.'

'Not while you've got my money,' I thought.

'Just a few more, and if the last group don't appear over that hill, I'll come with you.' I won back a couple of pounds and decided to settle. The Japanese were still not in sight.

'Look,' I said, 'you shelter by that tree again; I'll run back to the top of the hill. If they're not in sight, we're going in.'

'Thank you, sir,' he whispered through cracked and now purple lips.

I jogged to the top of the 16th fairway. There was no sight of the customers. That was it, I turned back towards the green. That was when I spotted the three Japanese huddled under the face of a high grass bunker to the right of the fairway, to escape the icy gale.

One looked up and from blue-tinged lips he called out, 'Are you two never going to finish this bruddy hole?!'

38

---•---

THE RYDER CUP

I would dearly love to write of my experience as a player in the Ryder Cup, but lack of that particular ability made that an impossible dream. However, I was able to achieve at least some participation in the capacity of referee and observer in three matches in the series from 1973 to 1977, before my position at Woburn caused me to leave my official position with the PGA.

Strangely enough, having represented Hertfordshire and Bedfordshire on the Southern Section and on the Executive Committee, I moved to the Duke of Bedford's new club, only to find it was in Buckinghamshire, and that county already possessed a well-established representative.

Only a home country official can referee; those on the away team can be observers. In 1973 at Muirfield I was sent out as an understudy to referee Hugh Lewis, who was then the professional at Altrincham and one of the funniest men I have ever met. An excellent player himself, Hughie has opted for a quieter life lately – a great pity, for there is no funnier a raconteur anywhere.

Ryder Cup referees take charge of their matches armed with a list of items. The R&A Rule Book, the USPGA Rule Book and the Ryder Cup Rule Book. They also have a card of the course to record the score, a long piece of string to measure any disputed putts, a megaphone to call out the result of each hole, and of course, a pencil.

Hughie was down to referee the opening match, which included Arnold Palmer. Both tee-shots lay fairly adjacent on the 1st fairway, so Hughie handed me the megaphone and stepped forward to decide who would play first, normally a referee's job.

'Where are you going?' snorted Palmer, hitching up his pants and glaring at my man.

175

'Just going to see who's to play first,' was the reply. Palmer glared at him: 'I'll decide that, it's him to play!' was all he said. Hughie went unusually quiet and rejoined me.

On the final day of that series I refereed a match between Brian Huggett and Homeros Blancas. The Welshman was 2-down but had a run of six consecutive 3s. to win the match.

At Laurel Valley in 1975 I was an observer, and what I did observe was how wet America can be. Parking attendants allowed the arriving spectators to drive along the metal strips to their allotted parking spot, at which point they turned their huge cars onto the grass, where they sank up to their axles. In the evening they towed them all back onto the track by means of a large tractor.

How different Ryder Cup matches are today. Then we went out knowing we would lose: it was only a matter of by how many games.

By 1977 at Royal Lytham and St Annes some of the players who have changed all that were beginning to emerge. One of them whose match I was due to referee on the final day in his first Ryder Cup: that was Nick Faldo playing against Tom Watson, probably the world's best player at that time.

As a preparation, on Day One, I was assigned to Tony Gray of the PGA, who would take me around in the fourball match just to give me confidence. His match included Britain's Ken Brown and Mark James against America's Hale Irwin and Lew Graham.

'There's nothing to it, Alex, the rules are mostly common sense and these guys know them all anyway,' proclaimed the confident Irishman.

The disputes started half-way down the 2nd hole. There were twenty-two of them in all, of which I thought I knew the answers to only two, and both times I was wrong. The round took 5½ hours, including arguments, and the Americans won, Ken Brown's chip from behind the last green for a tie stopping on the very lip of the hole.

Back in the hotel my great friend Ken Swayne, with whom I have shared many golfing adventures, tried to comfort me: 'After dinner we'll have a read through the rule books, then in the morning at breakfast I'll ask you a couple of questions and you'll answer them just like that!' snapping his fingers. We did, and then I couldn't.

The Watson–Faldo match was actually minutes late going from the tee, the only match held up by the late appearance of its referee: I was in the toilet.

176

I needn't have worried, I needed not my rule books, or my string; and the noise around the greens was so deafening they couldn't hear my announcements anyway, so I just pretended to be shouting.

We were round in 2½ hours of birdies and eagles, and Faldo won on the last putt.

39

BBC TELEVISION

It was at the time·of the 1977 Ryder Cup that I had joined Woburn. My old club, Ashridge, had acted in a most considerate fashion by allowing me to spend, for a period of six months, 3½ days there and 3½ days at Woburn. This would give me the chance of continuing to earn a living with them and allow Woburn to get nearer to having its full facilities.

It was shortly after this that David Coleman sent me to BBC's Slim Wilkinson for a trial at Birkdale. I can hardly describe the feelings I had when I stuck the green BBC TV sticker in my car window that would allow me through all the normal car parks right to the commentary area. I think I had it glued to the glass for over a week before the event and for about two weeks after it. Then, of all things, the day before I drove to Birkdale I developed the worst sore throat and running nose I'd ever had, and anyone who spends his life standing out on freezing practice grounds knows all about those.

I've always thought how funny it is that when, as a teaching Pro, you make your way from the shop past the Clubhouse, when the sun is beating down from clear blue skies, there is the smell of newly cut grass and with you your new pupil who looks like Miss World, there is always a mass of envious faces peering at you from the members' bar. You can almost hear the envious remarks: 'And he calls that work!' Yet when the icy rain is battering against your buckling umbrella as you head out with someone that looks like one of Cinderella's sisters, all you see are backs of their heads. No one wants to know of your conditions.

I arrived at the Production Caravan, the place where plans are drawn up, and where I have enjoyed much laughter, especially when Alliss is in one of his funny moods and reads aloud his daily viewers' correspondence, which apparently, according to the reader has at the end of every one a postscript expressing their opinions of that Scottish twit. It is the caravan where our day begins and ends.

I felt that day, though I'd never been in one, that it would end for me there and then as I coughed and spluttered my way towards the door. Thank goodness Peter, whom I had admired as a golfer for many years and then as a commentator, though I had only met him occasionally, spotted me and realized the trouble I was in.

He introduced me, kindly pretending I was an old buddy and suggested to the management that I shouldn't go on trial yet, but have a day or two to get better.

Thankfully, that was agreed and I was allowed to sit in a corner of the Commentary Box and listen to how it was done. People don't realize just what goes on in the commentator's earphones as he tries to talk; I felt convinced after that first day I'd never make it. Directors; producers; assistants; counting down numbers; linking with London; shouting at cameramen, then praising them; video tapes running who's on the odds, who's on the evens? I was so relieved when Harry Carpenter took the show off the air, as he's done every time since, on the dot of the count-down's zero.

Days Two and Three became more understandable. I listened to the ease of Peter and noted how he only talked as he would if he were on the course close to the player and how he stopped talking as soon as the club went near the ball. Then as they putted, even though on a green miles away, he would whisper just as greenside spectators do. Here was a golfer talking to golfers whilst golfers whose circumstances and emotions he understood golfed.

On the Saturday night, as the show closed down, the Director asked who would sit in on Alex's trial next morning at 10 a.m. Before anyone could utter a sound Peter said, 'I'm doing it.'

He and I shared a few early finishers over the closing holes, and he made it easy for me. Then they let me record a piece which was put on the highlights that evening, and I was promised my name would go up on the closing captions that night. I think I phoned and told everyone I knew, but the BBC forgot to include me.

Before leaving, I picked up my cardboard lunch box and had everyone sign it, and it is in my study today. Henry Cotton is boldly written, mind you, and so it should be – Henry had been inside it so many times. I had noticed during my three days of waiting and regaining my health that each time the kitchen staff delivered the lunch boxes, which usually contained something like a chicken salad, a meat pie, and either a Mars bar or a Kit-Kat, Henry would take a break and go to the toilet. On his return, when all were in action

179

on air, he would open the lids of all the boxes and pocket everyone's chocolate. Each of the boxes had a commentator's initials on it so that he could eat something when he felt inclined, then go back later for more.

I recall on Day Three Peter, who enjoys picking away, rummaging through box PA: 'I remember the days when the BBC could afford a bar of chocolate.'

'So can I,' replied Harry. 'Economizing again, I suppose.' Meanwhile Henry munched away; earphones are marvellous things to hide behind, if you wish to pretend you don't hear what is being said.

I said nothing, but on Day Four, when Henry excused himself and followed the kitchen assistant through the door, I borrowed a felt pen and scored out all initials and wrote HC on all the boxes. Henry came back, looked, said nothing, took one of the boxes and sat down.

'Peter,' said Harry, 'they must have overheard us yesterday; look, I've got a Mars bar!'

At Birkdale, Nick Faldo had won his first PGA Championship, and I had got into the team and, overjoyed, was told that I had to report at St Andrews for the Open Championship, which I did.

Again my cold returned, as it did for every event for almost two years until my Dr Evans, a member of Ashridge, told me it was a psychological cold. It stopped in 1980, the day he told me.

At St Andrews my cold turned out to be a blessing in disguise. The roof of the new Old Course Hotel, which projects into the dog-leg of the 17th hole, had been chosen as the site for the commentary box, and without doubt it offered spectacular views right up the closing holes and into that lovely old town.

Unfortunately – and I cannot give the true cause – the vents from the toilets in the entire building had been incorrectly taken up inside the building and allowed to escape at roof level. On the cold windy day the contractors built the commentary box, there were few using the hotel and no one thought twice about the grills over which the box was constructed.

That year St Andrews broke all previous records for the Open, a feat equalled by the lavatories of the Old Course Hotel. Because of my psychological nose I didn't notice much on the first day, but the others certainly did. By Day Two even my nose, which not only suffered its temporary ailment but was protected by being severely bent on a rugby pitch at Tradegar, gave up the resistance. The commentary box was humming, not with activity, but with stench.

On that day, the sun came out and St Andrews sweltered. People enjoying the hospitality in the hotel below our seats were having a ball; queues formed at the toilets. Many storeys above, our box was filling with flies.

This may seem an unfortunate place to point out that it was then, for the first time, I met Peter's lovely wife, Jackie, but what a blessing she was! She produced one of those roll-on perfumed deodorants, which she applied vigorously under our noses every few minutes as we went though the first two ten-hour days. Scotland's long summer evenings permit play well into the evening.

By Day Three the stench was unbearable; complaints had been lodged, but to no avail. I recall thinking how glamorous a profession I had joined. All those who performed the other skilful tasks in the box, the graphics and scorers, now had cotton masks tied around their faces.

The other Cotton in question had had enough and he made a phone call to some high place in London, they do say at Government level. When we arrived for the fourth and final day, there towards the top of the building, a whole area of the brickwork had been smashed away and huge venting pipes were secured, directed towards the end of the building.

I believe all has now been permanently put right, but we have never worked from that vantage point again.

Having referred to Peter Alliss' readings of viewers' correspondence and the humour that it, together with the unwritten lines he reads out, brings to the relaxed atmosphere of the production caravan, there is nevertheless a serious aspect to the viewers' letters, many of which can be quite hurtful.

Strangely enough, when Independent Television was covering golf, we at the BBC used to receive many letters of praise, comparing us with the 'other side'. Then, when ITV gave up covering the sport, the public, who had no one else to complain about, turned their venom, which apparently has to be directed somewhere, at us. Fortunately we all still receive many letters of support, which outweigh the others; nevertheless, some do sting when they arrive just before you are going on the air.

Many refer to expressions you use; often they criticize your repetition, asking, 'Why must you tell us this is so-and-so when you have been covering him for the past six holes.' They don't realize the commentator is required continually to update the player in question, as well as where he is on the course, because the BBC method of showing 'highlight' programmes in the evening is built upon actual commentary and not that dubbed onto an edited film; therefore the past six holes the writer refers to might not be seen on that evening's showing, which is why we continually update.

The technical criticisms do not worry the commentator too much, for viewers cannot be expected to understand what goes on behind the scenes. What can hurt is when the person is attacked. In my own case it is my accent that causes more critical correspondence, and all of it from Scotland.

It was the morning after my first day on the air from the roof of the Old Course that I first experienced I had a problem, first, in the repetition of certain words and then in the way I pronounced them. It was in a mood of great elation that I made my way from my hotel to the Production Caravan. The first day, when our commentary system had given each of us a group of nominated matches, which meant that whenever one of your players appeared on the screen you switched on, I had been given only three groups to cover, as my breaking-in process. The first contained a fairly unknown American, Tom Kite. In my second group a young English-based golfer from Kenya, Gary Cullen, and in my third a young Spaniard, Seve Ballesteros, all of whom scored 67s, making them joint leaders and giving me a huge chunk of the highlights programme. I was delighted; even though it was next day that they decided to change to the system when one covers the odd holes and the other the evens, they had realized the danger of the previous method of coverage.

Walking towards the complex, feeling full of the joys of spring, I was joined by Lionel and Betty, a dear couple who have taken care of golf commentary teams for many years, Betty determined to fill you full of tea and chocolate biscuits.

'Our landlady thinks you're very good.' I felt even better still. 'It's just the way you say tre-MEN-dous.' Betty exaggerated the Scottish emphasis of the middle syllable. 'And you say it so many times.' Now I was unsure.

When I got into my chair in the commentary box, the smell meant nothing; I asked the director if he had heard my 'treMENdouses'. He had noticed a few.

'Do me a favour,' I begged. 'if I do it again, warn me.' I had now made up my mind I wouldn't say it again.

As I started my stint that morning, it was Peter Thomson driving at the 1st, his ball coming to rest just short of the Swilken Burn.

'What a treMENdous tee shot.' This was greeted by a whole chorus of voices from the scanner: 'You've done it again, Alex.' I was now paranoid about it, and determined to eliminate all three-syllable descriptive words from my vocabulary, even to the extent of writing out a list of one- and two-syllable options and sticking it to my monitor: FINE, SPLENDID, SUPER would replace fanTAStic, inCREdible and, of course, the now hated treMENdous.

By the time I had made my return to Woburn and headed to the teaching ground to join a pupil, I had regained my confidence. As I approached he said, 'My wife thinks you sound great on the television.' I felt much better; this was the recognition I needed. 'Except when you use that word all the time.' My moment of joy was deflated.

'I don't use it any more, I shall never say treMENdous ever again.'

'That's not the word, it's the way you say PURRfict!'

The Scots think I am trying to be an Englishman; they don't realize that when you leave your country at the age of nineteen and live in another for almost twice that long certain changes will take place in your pronunciation, and though the English think I am very Scottish, many Scots don't agree. One wrote to me recently and asked, 'Why don't you pronounce BURDIE and FURST correctly? If they were meant to be "birdie" and "first" they'd be spelt with I's and not U's!' And he was serious; the rest of his letter is unprintable.

———————●———————

There is never the deliberate intention to lose your home tongue; indeed I never thought I had until I went home to Musselburgh a few years ago and fancied a really fresh piece of fish for lunch. The local harbour of Fisherow, which when I was a boy was home to a marvellous fleet of some fifty or so timber-hulled fishing boats, but now sadly has hardly any, did at least still have a fresh-fish stall by the jetty.

I drove up in my big shiny Jaguar car and approached the counter: 'Could I have a couple of large, really fresh filleted haddocks, please?'

'Aye sir, ye can that,' said the fishmonger, selecting the two largest fish from his display and proceeding to weigh them and roll them up in paper. 'That's a braw car ye have there, I expect ye'll be up here oan yer hoalidays?'

I realized then what the letter-writers meant; here I was only a few hundred yards from where I was brought up, and he thought I was English. 'Well,' I replied, handing over the money, English pound notes, which suddenly felt dirty, 'I am visiting, but I did live just across there.' I pointed towards the town. 'In fact, my Granny used to sell fish right about where we're standing.'

He looked hard at me, disbelief in his eyes.

'What wid yoor name be then?'

'My name's Hay, Alex Hay.'

'You're a Hay?' – the uncertainty was still there. 'Wha' wis yoor faither then?'

'Ma faither – my dad was Willie Hay.'

'You're Wullie Hay's laddie?' He was now believing me; he started to unwrap my fish. 'Jimmy,' He called out to his accomplice, 'this is Wullie Hay's laddie; get oot the fresh fish.' He turned to me: 'Ye'll no be havin' this, this is fur they English!'

40

---•---

A TRILOGY OF CARS

I have always been one who makes that boring and usually untrue boast that all I need from a car is that it gets me from A to B – although I do have one or two other requirements, such as that it is extremely comfortable, that it goes fairly quickly, and that it is safe.

During my career I have used, and probably abused, many cars, but of all I have distinct memories of only three: a 1936 Morris 10, a silver-grey Morgan sports car, and a Ford Granada.

In 1957, when I was interviewed by the Committee and Ladies' Captain of East Herts, I assured them that I would be able to commute by car from the tiny farmyard cottage Ann and I rented near Potter's Bar in a car I planned to buy.

Although this was not quite accurate, for I held no driver's licence, I was happy that, should I be given the appointment, I could very quickly remedy the situation. Britain was in the midst of the Suez crisis and petrol was rationed, so driving tests were postponed. This meant that, provided you had sufficient experience of driving in the company of a qualified driver you might attach 'L' plates and drive where you wished.

My position confirmed, I rang Reg Taylor, who had been the Senior Assistant at Potter's Bar with Bill Shankland but was now in his own post at Stanmore Golf Club. Reg was about to purchase a new car and his old Morris 10 was to be sold for the princely sum of £75. Not only was I able to buy it for this price, he would provide sufficient tuition to see me safely to Hertford and back.

Reg's idea of how much instruction was necessary might have fallen short of that of the authorities, for he turned up fairly late on the Sunday evening, the eve of my first day at East Herts.

We sat in the car, in the darkness of the farmyard, whilst he guided me through the complexities of gear-change, as well as the workings of the clutch and brakes, which once mastered allowed me onto Hertfordshire's lanes.

Twenty terrifying minutes convinced Reg that I was proficient, and we returned to the farmyard. I paid over one-third of our worldly goods, and he set off for the bus stop, on foot.

I suppose I sat in the car for the best part of an hour practising gear-changing, but without switching on the engine; then, because I was going to drive to work next day, I decided to risk my first solo run. It was when the engine was running that I realized that we had not gone backwards during my lesson.

No doubt anyone who has learned to drive has experienced the difficulty of reversing: it is where to turn your head to gain the best view of the rear. This is made more difficult when it is black as ink outside, and 1936 cars had no reversing lights.

I let out the clutch and back we went; I was twisting inwards, attempting to see from the glow of my tail lights where I was going. There came a sickening crunch; the car lurched to a stop.

I had almost missed the farmer's 1938 Austin. My front bumper had hooked beneath his rear wing and removed it completely, though it was hardly damaged, from his car.

I was momentarily tempted to become a hit-and-run driver, but decided to own up, and carried his mudwing to the farmhouse door. His surprise and horror at having a piece of his car handed to him was only matched when he heard I was about to drive to work in the morning. I was able to offer the name of a good welding company in Potter's Bar, as well as the cost of the repair, and he good-naturedly accepted this. I returned to my machine, drove it the twenty yards back to where I had started it and parked. My solo mission of forty yards completed my training.

Unlike today, when Professionals' Shops are expected to open at least twelve hours a day and 364 days a year, except in a Leap Year, when they do 365, then it was acceptable to close for lunch – especially on a Monday, when at East Herts there was no catering, it being the Steward's day off.

We locked up the shop, a tiny wooden hut where the other two-thirds of our worldly goods were on display, and Ann and I drove to Hertford to a lunch room. Luckily I found an excellent parking spot right outside the front door and we settled down to enjoy lunch. I was still shaking a bit, not only from my first solo drive but from my first lesson, Mrs Noble having been taken off to hospital.

Halfway through our meal a very large constable came through the doorway and after a discussion with the owner made the announcement: 'Will the owner of CLU 423 please make himself known.'

To this day I am hopeless at remembering my car's number; as for my Morris 10, I'd hardly seen it in daylight. We carried on eating. He left.

A short time passed and he came in again; this time the Manager approached me and suggested that the offending vehicle might be mine since it was parked between two sets of traffic lights opposite the main junction with Hertford High Street. This was illegal.

I joined the officer on the pavement and apologized for my inexperience. He had no wish to discuss this in Hertford High Street and suggested I get in the car and reverse it into the lane; then we would discuss the matter.

I got in, and he moved into the centre of the street to halt the traffic for my manoeuvre. That was where I left him; instead of attempting for the second time going backwards, I shot off down the High Street with him running after me. I knew there was a roundabout at the end of the street and around it I went, passing him on my return journey and parking as requested in the lane, where I was severely reprimanded.

That evening, having made it successfully to and from my new job, I decided that after supper I would practise. This time, on the advice of Ann, I made certain that the farmer had not parked behind me as on the previous night. This time I opened the driver's window and leaned well out, a technique a friendly member at my new job had advised me to try.

There was no question that this gave me much better vision of behind and to the right. Unfortunately not of behind, and to the left. There came the familiar sickening crunch.

I carried the rear offside mudwing to the farmhouse, but hid it out of sight before ringing the bell.

'You had me worried for a moment, I thought you'd come to tell me you'd knocked off the wing again. I spent all afternoon getting it welded back on.'

'No, I didn't,' I replied.

'Thank goodness for that! Hang on, I'll get you the bill.'

He returned and handed me the invoice.

'No hard feelings,' he said, smiling. 'It can happen to anyone.'

'I'm glad you feel that way.' I handed him the other side of his car and paid him double.

I drove that little Morris 10 everywhere, often backwards, for two years and sold her for £50: my only expense, the price of two mudwings for an Austin.

———————————●———————————

At one stage in my career, I had just received a healthy cheque for a book; I felt a little bit of luxury was warranted. A member of Woburn, Mike Ivory, had in his garage an immaculate silver-grey Morgan sports car, which he very kindly suggested I should try for a day or two before considering purchasing it.

What a flyer it was, and with the roof off it was like being in a racing car! The day I tried it was the practice day for the girls in the Ford Ladies' Classic at Woburn, so, as I roared up the club drive, I could see the girls' heads turn. This was just the car for me. I shot round the flower-beds and swung into my parking spot, screeching to a halt.

At that moment a rather gorgeous American Pro-ette, her hair flowing down her back, almost reaching down as far as the hem of her mini skirt, flaunted towards me.

'Alex,' – I was no longer Mr Hay – 'might I sit in your car with you?' I couldn't believe my luck; I'd only had this sex machine for an hour and already I'd pulled a bird! 'You British Pros are incredible, and you even dye your hair to match your cars!'

Mike got his silver-grey Morgan back the same afternoon.

———————————●———————————

The last of the three cars that have left vivid impressions was a Ford. It goes without saying that being involved with television opens many doors and gives the opportunity to meet many nice and often helpful people.

One, by the name of Rex Holton, approached me and asked me if I would like to have a nice new Ford car. Obviously I enquired as to what was involved; after all, nice as many are, they do often possess ulterior motives.

There were no snags and apparently only two conditions. The first was that I must have painted along its sides that 'Alex Hay drives Ford from Hacfield'. 'Is that all I have to do?' It wasn't; what he also required was that at all televised golf events, particularly Open Championships, I should do all in my power to park it alongside 'PUT 3', Peter's Rolls-Royce, for everyone has a look at that one, so they'd see mine too. I agreed.

All went well until the 1979 Open, when Seve won in such a remarkable fashion. Often, towards the close of the Open, some kindly producer of champagne who might just accidentally have happened to get a mention during transmission turns up with a bottle or three so that we might toast the health of the Champion. That famous Sunday was no exception, and we were understandably a bit hyped up at Seve's win.

Finally, when we eventually left the box and descended the wooden staircase, at the bottom of which was the gleaming 'PUT 3', and tight beside it my blue Ford with its personal wording 'Alex Hay drives Ford from Hacfield', under it, in even larger letters, someone had aerosoled 'NEVER MIND, YOUR LUCK MIGHT CHANGE'.

It hasn't, I still drive Fords. However, without printing, it became a target for an over-zealous boy in a policeman's uniform, and I spent a year walking!

41

DOCTORS

When the 1979 Open started my Dr Evans had not yet told me of my psychological problem and I arrived with a streaming cold. So too, did Peter, his really serious, and in fact it caused him to pull out on the second day and return to his hotel.

There was one stage on the first day when he and I were on the same shift – commentators work in pairs at the Open on a shift system of something like two hours on and one off, sometimes overlapping. We were sitting one on each side of the scorer, who was frantically passing a box of tissues back and forth between us. It was soon used up.

There are very few things worse than a fit of coughing when you are either making a speech or doing a commentary, and Peter was hit by a fierce bout, so bad that he switched his mike off to stop it going round the world; he pushed his chair back and went to the door of the box and stood coughing his heart out to the amusement of the huge galleries in the grandstand into which our box was built.

I was on my own then, and I knew it was coming, even though I now know it was only in my mind: I was about to have another fit of coughing. At the time I was covering Brian Barnes, who was preparing to play a shot at the 2nd hole. Peter had stopped coughing and was gasping for air. I pulled back my little red switch that disconnects commentators from the viewers. Tears were in my eyes. 'Get Peter back, quick!' I spluttered.

Ricky Tilling, the Director, was shouting, and in our earphones we could sense his frustration: 'They've all gone dumb up there, say something, somebody!' I switched on again: 'Brian Barnes has about 150 yards to go.' The coughing started; I switched off.

'Get Peter,' I pleaded. They were dragging Peter to his chair; he looked awful as he slumped in it. 'Say something else,' pleaded Ricky. I switched on again, spluttering: 'He's using an 8 iron.' I switched off. The coughing was at its worst now. 'Is that it?' demanded Ricky. 'This is the Open Championship, and that's all he can say?'

I looked at Peter; could he take over? No, he was still 'wiring up' between sneezes. I drew breath and switched on as Brian struck: 'He's hit it up,' was all I got out. I knew I'd had it; so did the Studio Manager, who wrenched my mobile chair back from the bench; the mikes were all picking up the sound.

Peter was just about fit to start when Ricky pleaded again, 'Somebody say something, please!' Peter still choking, spluttered, 'It's down again.'

'So it should be, it's bloody well been up for five minutes!'

Harry rescued us by picking up the commentary and taking us through the break. Peter and I were leaning up against the outside walls coughing our hearts out, yet even then fans were reaching out to him with their autograph books.

We thought probably no one had noticed and we'd got away with it until I went into the chemist shop in St Anne's Square. Still wheezing, I asked the chemist if he could help. He replied, 'Yes, Mr Hay, I knew you or Mr Alliss would be in; I've prepared this for you, with my compliments!'

I am pleased to say that was the last year, touch wood, of coughing for the both of us, though we did have quite a scare about Peter's health in 1988. It was well reported and we all thought he had contracted pneumonia. Somehow he kept going but showed no sign of getting better, which was causing some concern all round.

Fortunately the cause was finally diagnosed to be psittacosis, a disease that comes from parrots, and Peter had given his children a bird for Christmas. Once diagnosed, and with Polly safely at the bottom of the garden, Peter immediately started to recover.

The day he actually realized that he was not going to die – and up till then he had not been too sure for several weeks – was the first day of the 1988 Open Championship once again at Royal Lytham and St Annes. It was about an hour before we were due to start our transmission and I was the only one in the caravan when he arrived.

'How do you feel?' I enquired, so used to getting a 'not so good' reply; but today was different: 'I feel great, what's more, since I haven't had a drink for over a month, you and I shall wander to the Bollinger tent.'

Getting from A to B with Peter during a championship takes ages: everyone wants to talk to him and have his autograph, and no one is refused.

Eventually we made it, and the hosts, always happy to see Peter, opened a bottle, which we sat out in the sun behind the marquee to enjoy.

I have found champagne in the morning very dangerous, especially before broadcasting. This I had found to my cost early in my career when Peter and Harry Carpenter had kindly introduced me to a very exclusive club, taking me to a small room inside the Payne's catering marquees where I met Gus Payne, the founder of the company. The debonair Gus had, for many years enjoyed a little smoked salmon and a bottle of champagne with Henry Longhurst just one hour before transmission. Peter and Harry had been invited to join the club, and now, with Henry gone, I was privileged to be a part of the elite gathering.

I have to admit that I was surprised to see how easily the champagne disappeared as memories were recollected, and, not wishing to be a spoilsport, I happily joined them – after all, if it made them as good as they were, it might help me!

About 10.55 a.m. we were to start broadcasting. At 10.45 a.m. someone suggested we'd better get back, so off we went, Peter signing his autographs and Harry too. We only just got into our seats in time and wired up. Our theme music was already playing; I felt strangely relaxed. The music stopped; Harry welcomed every-one to Wentworth in his normal fluent style and told them how play was progressing:

'Now we are going live to the 13th and our commentator is . . .'
– there's always a slight hesitation as Harry determines, by looking along the row to see who's on odd and who's on evens; one of us waves, – '. . . Alex Hay.' All I said was, 'Thank you, Harry,' and in my earphones our Director reacted instantly: 'He's pissed!' I tried to get through my next sentence as articulately as I could, feeling each word progressively slurring. 'So he is,' agreed the Producer. 'Bring in Peter.' Peter, like Harry, just flowed into action, whilst I sat there stunned. I vowed never again!

Although I found out years later that Slim and Ricky had been told where I'd gone and had rehearsed their act, I am still very wary and attend the morning meeting now with Gus' son, Alan; for sadly, like Henry, Gus is no longer with us, but the memories remain and are regularly reflected upon with great respect and affection.

So, with Peter now feeling much better, we settled to enjoy another cooling glass, mine remaining fairly full, whilst Peter's was

192

replenished freely. We were joined that morning by the R&A's Championship medical officer, Dr Mackenzie, a huge jovial Scot and a favourite of Peter's. Good reason for another bottle.

The subject of our conversation got to Musselburgh, when I discovered the doctor was one of the Queen's Archers, who, to this day turn out in their dark green uniforms with their high feathered bonnets, a tradition dating back centuries when Scotland's King tried to ban his soldiers from the game of golf and make them return to their archery practice.

Out of tradition, the Old Links of Musselburgh are closed for the day and the bowmen send arrows from their longbows some 200 yards to distant targets which they hit with great regularity; the winner is awarded with a Silver Arrow.

I was fascinated to meet the doctor, for, as a boy, I used to watch this tradition, at first because it interfered with my golf, but then out of fascination.

What a good story this would be, I thought, to tell the world when one of those occasions when 'everyone' is walking came up, and the director tells you from the scanner to 'waffle'.

We were joined by other friends, all happy to see Peter's return to normal, and another bottle was on its way.

'Peter,' I nudged him, 'don't you think we should go? We're on in ten minutes?'

'I'm not,' he replied. 'You're on the first shift with Bruce. I'm not till twelve.' He looked at his watch: 'You're going to be late!' he smiled. He really was returning to normal: 'Off ya go!'

We were about an hour into the show when Peter arrived, a happy, relaxed glow about his countenance; he was wiring up.

It was at that moment that one of those lulls in action that requires waffling occurred: no one was playing, everyone was walking, so I launched into my story about the R&A's medical officer. I had carefully involved Musselburgh's history – good stuff, I thought, for an Open Championship, especially about a Scottish King banning golf. Peter now had his earphones on and was checking his lunch box. That was the point where I announced that Dr Mackenzie was one of the famous Archers. Peter started whistling the theme tune to our longest running radio series. He was completely unaware, and as I struggled on about my Archer his whistling got louder; now everyone in the box was joining in.

I had to go on; I was only halfway through. My mischievous colleague had now realized a musical recital was taking place and had opened his internal mike, called 'the lazy' and now everyone

193

was whistling. Directors, John Shrewsbury and Alastair Scott, were dum de deum de dum de dumming. I thought I would never get through, the tears of laughter were streaming down my face.

42

———————●———————

COMMENTATING ABROAD

Of the interesting places television commentating has taken me Dubai must be one of the most fascinating. The Emirates' Golf Club appears out of the desert like a mirage as you are whisked by air-conditioned Mercedes cars along the straightest of strips of black tarmacadam. What in the distance appears to be a Bedouin encampment of half a dozen tents grows in size as your car speeds towards them; then you realize that their construction is not canvas but concrete and that each towers three storeys above the desert, housing one of the most luxurious clubhouses in the world.

As for the course, it was built directly from the desert with the aid of bulldozers, American technology, both in design and grasses, and a million gallons of desalinized water a day being pumped on to it. They set out to build a championship course from nothing and they have succeeded.

The story goes that when His Highness Sheikh Mohammed bin Rashid Al Maktoum was watching his horses run on television the horseracing kept being interrupted whilst golf was televised, first to his annoyance and then to his fascination. Surely if people could be more interested in chasing a little white ball about than watching horses run, he should be involved. He consulted his Yorkshire projects manager, a keen golfer by the name of Stephen Trutch, who like other ex-patriates played his golf on the other desert courses, carrying around a square of plastic grass from which they hit their shots. The result of their discussion started the ball rolling: Dubai would have the first all-grass course in that hemisphere.

An American architect by the name of Karl Litten was called in to make preliminary designs. When asked by the Sheikh how much it would cost to build a course there, Karl thought for a moment then, deciding to throw a fairly high price at the Sheikh, answered with a guess at 'about three to five million', waiting to see the reaction before adding pounds or dollars. The Sheikh stroked his beard for a moment, then replied, 'three hundred and twenty five million seems rather a lot.' Karl knew he was on safe ground, and plumped for pounds.

Strangely enough, the Sheikh's racing being interrupted by golfers was not dissimilar to our televised coverage of the opening event on his golf course being interrupted by another sport, that of camel-racing. I was invited by the man in charge of public relations, Terry Duffy, a former English League footballer, who does a marvellous job of promotion there, to join Renton Laidlaw, who makes Alan Whicker look like a stay-at-home, to provide commentary on an East versus West match which was to form the opening of the course. This would be preceded by a couple of days of Pro-Ams permitting local companies to participate.

From the palatial viewing areas of the Clubhouse you look out over an oasis of green fairways, huge lakes teeming with tropical fish, fountains throwing water a hundred feet in the air, so separating the approach to double greens; it makes a change from fir trees.

My first viewing of this breathtaking sight was interrupted when the commentary box was pointed out to me. It was out of keeping with the pure luxury of every other aspect. About 300 yards from the clubhouse stood a square white block of a building upon which sat a wooden box, with a roof and no windows.

My old friend, Ricky Tilling, now retired from the BBC, had been commissioned to provide the pictures and had arrived in Dubai some weeks earlier to set up the arrangements. Upon his arrival he was told that Dubai television, though they had never done golf, were in readiness. They had a couple of cameras and a few yards of cable to spare.

By the time Ricky had finished explaining their shortcomings, he was simply asked to write a list of what would be needed, where it could be found, and how much it would weigh. The answers were given and the 5½ tons were flown to the Emirates on their own airline – as simple as that!

'There has to be a scanner room' (the operations from where the entire visual part centres), 'and in this climate it must be air-conditioned.' What a pity Ricky didn't suggested the commentators might prefer air-conditioning too. It took six days to construct the white stone production building, with its air-conditioning, and an afternoon to build the wooden commentary box without. After three days up there the locals had named me Beau Geste.

On the first day of the Pro-Am event the thing they feared the most occurred: a sand-storm. It blew sand from the desert to the west right across the course to the desert on the east, all of it by way of my commentary box. I recall Ricky at the end of my earphones asking the engineers what was the funny whistling noise he could hear every time I spoke; it turned out to be the sand whistling across my teeth every time I uttered a sound.

Because there were no windows, all of the notes I had made ended up in the Gulf. My reading glasses, which are essential for viewing the monitor, blew off and broke across the bridge and had to be taped together for the rest of the event.

Six hours were done on each of the first two days; fortunately, on the second day the wind dropped and the heat of the sun could be felt. Lunch was delivered in a flat cardboard box, inside of which was what appeared to be a foil-covered pancake. Identification was not easy because the contents were covered by flies the moment the wrapper was opened. I grew of the opinion that this pancake-shaped bread which measured about a foot across, was so designed that you could roll some salad in one end which you ate, then by a skilful wrist action you could flick at the flies with the other.

Having somehow got through the two opening days, where amateurs whom I had never seen before struggled around this monster championship test, the official match day arrived, and so did Renton, and we settled down to cover golfers whom we both knew well. Just as things were hotting up we were instructed to bid farewell to viewers and introduce the camel-racing.

What the Sheikh's first impressions of golf were I know not but I know that I found their camel-racing about as exciting as watching paint dry – except, that is, for the last few minutes. Apparently camels do not like to pass the same place twice, so the track has to be straight – not easy since the race is over some fifteen miles.

At the start, about fifty of the beasts line up, taking up almost the entire width of the track, which consists of two parallel metal fences stretching the fifteen miles. Little lads, aged about ten, are velcroed onto the back of the camel. Strips of velcro on the seat of their pants clinging to matching strips on the camel's saddle so that they don't fall off. Then off they go, and they proceed in that long, slow, trotting gait of the ship of the desert.

Because of the duration of the race, there is time to show you the owners in the luxury of their pavilions watching the progress on television screens and instructing their trainers. Then you see rows of Mercedes and BMW cars which will be presented to trainers and the families of the jockeys who do well. Finally comes the closing

197

stages of the race, when the trainers speak to the little lads, who have close-circuit radios inside their helmets, and tell them where to aim and when to hit the mount. Then it all hots up and the commentator, who has never stopped for breath since the off, really does get carried away. Then it's all over. Then they show you a re-run. And after all that you return to the golf.

———————————●———————————

Another marvellous place to commentate is Hong Kong. I think what fascinated me most is how each new building on a tiny island is rising higher than the last one built. The place simply buzzes with commercialism until you can almost feel the vibration. Remarkably the scaffolding they still use on the outside of these towers is bamboo poles.

I don't know how the Chinese constructors feel when they go up these thirty- and forty-storey monsters, their lives depending upon bamboo tied together with bits of fibre, but if it's anything like what I felt climbing up the thirty-foot camera tower above the last green at Fanling, the word could be 'terrified'.

What a strange mixture of ancient and modern exists in the Royal Hong Kong Golf Club, which started its life in 1889 in very humble beginnings and has progressed through the century to be the hub of golf in Asia! Whilst you find corporate memberships being bought and sold for tens of thousands of pounds you still have, inside that lovely old pillared clubhouse, dormitories, identical to those of many old English boarding schools: six beds to a room with a small partition between them: at the end of the room a chest of drawers, each drawer numbered to match a bed, in which the occupant of the bed can place his belongings. From the corridor there is an ablutions room. To sleep at the club requires a payment of thirty Hong Kong dollars a night, about £2.00.

What impresses me most about golf clubs like the Royal Hong Kong is the marvellous comradeship. No doubt it comes because the members are mainly from foreign lands; and though they are very different lands, they are brought together by the fellowship of golf, the game which unites countries.

43

THE TEAM

It is annoying just how quickly time passes, and it is even more noticeable when working with the BBC team: you count back the years by the Open Championships. I often ask my golfing friends how long they think Peter Alliss has been involved and how long I have. The answer is generally ten or twelve years for Peter and four or five for me. They, and I, find it hard to believe Peter first became involved in 1961, and as for me 1978 seems just a season or two ago.

Our commentary team has remained almost unchanged since about 1980, when it became Harry Carpenter, Peter Alliss, Clive Clark, Bruce Critchley and myself, Tony Jacklin became involved in 1985.

Peter's playing skills made him one of the best British players of his time, with over twenty-five major professional and International Open titles to his credit, as well as a successful Ryder Cup career.

Clive, who joined the team about 1976, was then Professional at Sunningdale and, after a very successful amateur career where he gained Walker Cup honours, he turned professional and added a Ryder Cup place to his list. His 3rd-place finish in the Open at Hoylake must have been the highlight of his professional career.

Bruce is another from Sunningdale, but as a Club member, and he also enjoyed a successful amateur career culminating in Walker Cup honours.

There is no real need to describe Tony's career: those halcyon days in the late sixties and early seventies when he held the Open Championships of Great Britain and America at the same time, then his new-found career as Ryder Cup Captain, are known to all.

As for myself, like Peter, I had no career as an amateur; financially I couldn't afford to stay as one, and all I could see from the outset was being a professional. Unlike Peter, my playing career was limited by many factors, a combination of physical, mental and circumstantial. Winning a few Alliance events, the odd course record and the odd mention in despatches about sums it up although one Glasgow newspaper did report me as being leading money-winner worldwide in 1978.

I had gone to a Pro-Am in Nassau the first week in January and won the two opening events played prior to the main competition. I think I collected about £500, and this was picked up by the newspaper hungry for golf news at this, their quietest time of year. The fact that Jack Nicklaus overtook me by £44,500 two days later changed nothing. I still claim that title.

Another claim I am happy to make is my association with many excellent players in a teacher/pupil relationship, and I gain immense pleasure now from their success.

As for Harry, well his claim to golfing fame is his membership of Dulwich and Sydenham and Royal St George's at Sandwich, and, of course, the respect he is held in by all the players he interviews and introduces to the viewing public.

I first realized just how good Harry is as a 'link man': introducing the programme, updating the play, keeping cool when most of us are panicking, when working at Muirfield on the coverage of the Walker Cup.

As we were going into a lunch break, and Harry had once more successfully closed the morning show on zero of the countdown, his counterpart on the American television team had arranged to tape an introduction, which would be added to their recorded highlights to be shown later that evening in America. Our cameraman on our gantry by the doorway of our elevated box would film the 'intro' and our people down below would record it for him.

As our American friend was being powdered and made up, idiot boards were being written up to remind him of his lines. 'Alex' – he called me over – 'you come from here, don't you? What's this river behind us?'

'That's the Firth of Forth!' I replied, fascinated at the preparation. I'd never seen Harry being tarted up like this.

Finally they were ready to roll. A man with a clapper-board slammed the top down.

'Take one!'

'Hi, folks, I'm speaking to you from Scotland, from Muirfield, home of the Honourable Company of Edinburgh Goffers – SHIT!'

'You missed the 'L' out!'

'Take two!'

'Hi, folks! I'm speaking to you from Scotland from Muirfield, home of the Honourable Company of Edinburgh Golfers.' His smiled broadened, he was through the worst. 'Behind me you can see the Forth of Firth – damn it!'

Some of us were trapped in the box, not wishing to excuse our way past the large group working on this production. We had thought, even after our long morning session there would be plenty of time for a toilet break after the few minutes this 'link' would take.

It was when 'Take Ten' was clocked up and cocked up that we made a break for it; some of us felt as though our back teeth were under water, and could wait no longer. They were still at it when we returned.

Everyone was so engrossed that we hadn't noticed the first of the afternoon matches was actually on the 1st tee. Suddenly our own Stage Manager called out, 'Quick Harry, wire up, we're on.' We all dived in; our music was actually playing.

'Cue Harry.' Harry started.

'Good afternoon, welcome to Muirfield, home of the Honourable Company of Edinburgh Golfers.'

We were off. We do, of course, enjoy a marvellous team spirit on the golf coverage, from the cameramen who pick up those balls in the sky, often in atrocious conditions, some of whom will wait for you to leave the box in the evening to ask what it was you were pointing out about so-and-so's swing. Many of them are keen golfers and wish to learn, as are the engineers who put it all together, yet listen intently all of the time.

Beside the commentators sit the scorers who take such a pride in the way they produce their scoresheets, many of which are auctioned later for charities. Computers have been tried, but they have not yet found one that taps you on the shoulder and points out some interesting fact worth mentioning.

I usually have Neville looking after me, a huge man who looks like an opera singer, with a more than healthy appetite, who sits and eats everything I'm not allowed to. When he points to a player's score, you believe it; his great hand covered in jewels and Rolex never misses.

Behind us sits the graphics team who provides information like the player's current score before the ball hits the bottom of the cup, as well as the ever-changing leader boards.

Beneath us, though not geographically, is where the voices in the earphones seem to come from; they are actually often 100 yards away in the 'scanner' looking at the cameramen's offerings to the production team. Girls changing the pictures as instructed on a massive and complex switchboard. There are people constantly changing the depth of colour as the ball drops from the bright sky to the shade of the ground. Sound engineers bringing in the noise of club meeting ball and comments from players. Others turning in one commentator who speaks quietly, then quickly changing for another who is loud.

Last but not least there are the 'chiefs', the directors and producers and their assistants, who conduct the entire orchestra, and who by their attitude can make or break a commentator.

I joined the team in 1978 when the director was Slim Wilkinson and the producer was Ricky Tilling, and there was an extremely happy team spirit which showed in the way everyone worked.

That spirit is back again under the direction of John Shrewsbury, working with Alastair Scott and Fred Viner – all fanatical and stylish golfers. Sadly there was a spell between those teams where much of the happiness went out of the production and being there wasn't quite as it should have been. Fortunately that is all over now, and the Production Caravan is a happy place to be; this is reflected in the presentation.

———————●———————

It would be wrong to discuss the commentary team without mentioning that remarkable American Mark McCormack, for, though he only works on the Open Championship and the Suntory World Matchplay, he is certainly a valued member.

Mark spends most of each of the mentioned events entertaining clients and potential clients and when we who are not so privileged get our regular invitation to lunch, signing the visitor's book is like adding your name to *Who's Who*, so full is the marquee of household names.

Our Director co-operates by giving Mark his schedule in advance so that he can plan ahead, with the result he turns up in the box about one minute before he is due on the air and has gone thirty seconds after fulfilling his stint. Why does he do it? He certainly doesn't need the money, he certainly cannot afford the time; he, like the rest of us, just loves it!

I have had the pleasure of sharing many stints with Mark, who is a very gracious person. I recall one day at the Open, he arrived looking very tired, a combination of jet lag and pressure of work; we were wired up and ready to roll when, due to a transmission change, the Director informed us we would not go on for thirty minutes.

Mark turned to me: 'Alex, I'm a bit tired, if you'll excuse me I'll just have a nap. With that he rested his head on his forearms on the bench and went out like a light.

I recall thinking mischievously that I might let him sleep in, recalling the story of Henry Longhurst, who, after a good luncheon, had dozed off in his chair and was gently snoring when through his earphones came the 'Cue Henry'. Henry woke with a start, grunted a couple of times, reached out, picked up a glass and started speaking into it. Whether true or false I don't know, but I thought I'd test Mark's reaction to a sharp awakening.

Twenty-nine minutes and thirty seconds later Mark sat up, picked up his mike and asked, 'Are we ready to go?'

One of the most common statements made to commentators is how easy it must all be: how else could it all sound so relaxed? I even received a letter from a hospital complimenting me for solving problems of patients suffering from insomnia. The nurses allowed them to watch the highlights show late at night and my voice put them all to sleep.

However there are the odd hair-raising moments that get the adrenalin going, apart from the start of every programme, when everyone gets just a little edgy. Don't ever believe anyone who tells you he doesn't: it's just like making an after-dinner speech. When the Master of Ceremonies pulls the chair out from beneath you, if you don't feel on edge you must be too drunk to talk.

On my second season with the team I was asked to come in early on Day One of the Martini Tournament at Wentworth, our first event of the year. When I asked why, I was told that there were six people who felt they could do the job better than me and they were all having a trial. I was taken aback, especially when I saw the six waiting by the Production Caravan: they were well known writers and actors. This was to be the end of my career on television.

I was to do the job with them, two at a time, that Peter had done with me at my trial at Birkdale, and talk through a few matches.

In they came, one on each side, fairly relaxed and full of confidence. Unlike the advantage my heavy cold had given me, three days of listening and learning, each was on for his first time with no idea of what it is like when all hell is let loose in your ears and you are expected not to listen to what is none of your business but never miss what is. Within minutes they all wished they had either never written in or allowed another to do so on their behalf.

It was on my first break in transmission, about noon, that I called in at Wentworth's Golfers' Bar and found all six sitting with brandies, all still grey at the gills.

44

———————•———————

LEARNING THE TRADE

One fairly exciting moment came the year the BBC took over the coverage of the Benson and Hedges Tournament at that superbly maintained golf course at Fulford.

Because I had never visited that Club, I travelled up a day earlier than normal; we usually get there for the 3 p.m. rehearsal the day before transmission. I was walking with Seve's game, enjoying watching him and learning the course, when I was approached by a young, out of breath, technician:

'Alex, will you come back to the Clubhouse, we're going on the air!'

'No we're not, not 'til tomorrow.'

'All the cricket's been wiped, we're on in half an hour.'

We were both out of breath by the time we reached the commentary box, which was still being assembled when I'd passed by earlier. Mounting the stairs to the top of the grandstand, I was stopped at the doorway; they hadn't completed the work. There were only a couple of planks across the scaffolding to get to the bench.

Once wired up, I spoke to the Director.

'Alex? Thank goodness we found you. We go on air in five minutes. You got all you need?'

'Well, I have no scoring system.'

'There isn't one. We've got someone parked on the A64 with a phone in his car. He'll ask the players what they are when they cross the road and phone in.'

'There are no scorers up here.'

'We'll get you a pencil and paper. Anything else?'

With two minutes to go (those gallant cricket commentators were still talking to give us time) Clive Clark arrived. He was immediately hooked up, an extra plank was added for him to stand on, then we went on air.

At 2.30 p.m. Harry Carpenter drove in through the Clubhouse gates, where he was greeted by the officials.

'Welcome, Mr Carpenter. The show's going well.'

'No, we're not on until tomorrow,' replied Harry. 'They're just rehearsing.'

The attendant pulled back the flap of his tent, where a portable television was showing our programme. Harry suddenly felt quite ill: he had come a day late. He parked the car and rushed to join us. Another plank was added.

Within seconds, Harry was connected, and no sooner had he informed downstairs he was here he was cued in, summing up play from our scraps of paper.

Considering none of the cameramen had ever seen Fulford, it was considered that a 5½-hour non-stop programme was one of the best rehearsals we ever had.

———————————●———————————

Another first came on our first visit to the Wilmslow Club, near Manchester, and on Day One we started the show with Peter on the odds and myself on the evens. Peter had taken the match, including Sandy Lyle, Des Smith and José Maria Canizares, down the 1st.

It was as they made their way towards the 2nd tee that all the monitors in the commentary box went down. We had no pictures at all, and assumed there was a power cut and all had gone.

'Alex, aren't you going to say something?'

'We've no pictures!'

'We have down here.'

That was when I was more than grateful that I had been trained by Bill Shankland to understand swings, for they calmly informed me that they would tell me who was at the ball, then I could describe the play from there.

One by one I introduced the players and advised the viewer what to look for in their swings, where the ball was likely to fly, and what hazards each must look out for. Then I heard the crack as club hit ball; fortunately, all three balls only just escaped the hazards I had mentioned.

The next problem was what to do whilst they walked: there was no sense in joining another game. The solution was slow motions

206

of each swing, with descriptions of each. The address position, the hold at the top, then the downswing followed by the pose at the finish.

That got them as far as the second shots, when we went through the same routine. Almost fifteen minutes passed without pictures. When they regained them the players were on the green; it felt like fifteen hours.

———————●———————

I shudder when I think of the mistake I made in the closing stages of the 1979 Open that cost viewers seeing Ben Crenshaw, who was joint leader at the time, finishing the crucial 17th hole which cost him the Championship.

Ben had driven into a grassy hollow to the right of the 17th, my hole. At the same time Seve Ballesteros was flashing his ball into the car park at the 16th, Mark's hole. I was engrossed, as I suppose all the golfing world was, at Seve's cavalier performance, and whilst the activity amongst the cars was taking place I committed the cardinal sin of missing a piece of information that I should have heard, that the video machine was recording Crenshaw's record shot, with the result that when I was cued in, I did not realize I was talking over a taped piece. Ben was trying for a long second, taking a risk, in the hope he might reach the green. He pulled it away to the left into awful trouble.

We then went back to see Seve's brilliant shot from the car park.

'Cue Alex,' Came Ricky Tilling's excited instructions; everyone gets up-tight at the end of a great Open. 'Crenshaw's fourth.'

How could that be, I remember thinking, he's only just had time to walk from his second shot. There were the missing few minutes held by our video machine that I could not account for.

'This is Crenshaw's third,' I announced.

'It is his fourth,' called Ricky.

I pulled my lazy switch and informed them that he'd only played three.

'Cue Mark, Seve at the 16th green.' Mark came into action and for a moment my conversation was put aside. Seve holed.

Back we went to the 17th green.

'Cue Alex, Crenshaw's 5th.'

I pulled back my lazy: 'It's only his 4th,' I insisted.

By now my advisors were either becoming unsure themselves, or sick fed-up: 'Go back to the tee.'

We went back to the tee, where I picked up Seve, and we never returned to the green to see poor Crenshaw take his six.

Fortunately, Peter, who was covering the final hole, was able to establish the facts and no more was said – not, that is, until dinner that evening. One of the great things about the team is that everyone knows the other is trying his best and no one has to be told of his mistake. He knows himself, and he suffers.

However, after the meal I took Ricky on one side and apologized. It was accepted. Then I made my second major mistake of the day when I said, 'I suppose my inexperience shows; it's having no formal training.' Ricky exploded: 'No training? No formal training? You've had a year with the best team in the world! Don't ever say you've had no training!'

I've never said that again, not to anyone. The subject was never raised again.

———————————•———————————

Wentworth is one of the great tournament venues, such a great course and always a marvellous atmosphere. Many spectators go there so regularly they have their own favourite parking spot beneath some large tree (or they had before the gales of 1987), where annual picnics are held. It is fairly common for us, as we make our way to and from the commentary box, that we are invited to partake of a little refreshment and join in the fun.

Peter told me I should join him when we were invited to the back of a Bentley owned by Tom Blackwell, a famous name in golf in the Sunningdale/Wentworth area. It was a splendid do: excellent food and superb wine. Eventually it was time to return to work and we made our farewells.

I had turned to leave when there was a tap on my shoulder: it was our host.

'Listen, my boy,' his mouth was full of game pie: 'a piece of advice for you.' Crumbs were flying everywhere.

'My dear friend, Henry Longhurst always said that golf was a silent game, so why don't you shut up and let us enjoy it!'

It was another lesson worth learning.

———————————●———————————

During the opening days of my first Championship at St Andrews, the cameras were only covering holes 1, 2, 3 and 4, and from the 14th home – a fairly common practice until the closing day, when all 18 are shown.

I was enjoying my new-found career, and with nominated players I knew that none of mine were anywhere near coming into vision for ages yet.

Peter was busy waxing lyrical away in the next chair and, though I still had my earphones on, I was totally relaxed. My chair was on its hind legs, my feet up on the bench, munching away on a steak roll, and no doubt talking too much, which was probably getting on Peter's nerves.

Somewhere down below in the scanner, our lords and masters spotted that a cameraman, because there are no trees to impede the view, had zoomed away out into the country and from the strangest of angles picked up Baldoveno Dassu putting on a green. They decided, since little exciting was happening, to 'use it'.

'Cue commentator on Dassu.' I choked on the huge mouthful of steak and roll. Dassu was one of mine. My feet came down so fast, I spat out the food and grabbed for my mike.

'C'mon, commentator, wake up!'

I looked at the screen. As far as I was concerned, Baldoveno might just as well have been on the moon. I had no idea where he was. I didn't switch on.

'Say something! Who's doing Dassu?'

'Peter,' I pleaded, 'what hole is that?'

Peter sat, arms folded, looking straight ahead over his half glasses; his expression never changed.

'Find out for yourself, my boy. Find out for yourself!'

Baldoveno holed his putt.

In I went.

'That was Baldoveno Dassu putting.'

'Tell us what he scored!'

'Holing that made him —?' I couldn't find his name on my scoresheet. Neville had picked up Peter's humour and wasn't pointing.

'Has made him what?' someone screamed.

'One better than if he'd missed it.'

There was a moment's stunned silence; they returned to Peter's match. I had learned yet another lesson.

45

CLIVE

'Are you down there, Clive?' I wonder how many times Clive Clark has had that called out to him as he roams the fairways as BBC's man out on the course. What surprises me is how many think his is a simple task when it certainly is not. The best way to appreciate what another does for a living is to try it oneself, which I did a couple of times, and I certainly now understand the problems faced.

Clive has learned and developed his own skill and is able to make himself available for comment from the right place and at the right time. He is, of course, working with a sound assistant and keeps in constant contact with the Director. We are not invited to ask Clive his trademark question until we know he is in position and ready to reply.

To do this, except in emergencies, and unusual circumstances, Clive positions himself around the landing area of the key players' drives. Once the balls have landed, his job is to leave the sound assistant and go quickly to the balls and establish the order in which the second shots are to be played, the yard-age left to reach the green and the degree of difficulty of each shot.

By the time the players, who normally stride out, are approaching their balls, Clive joins his sound man and both move at least fifty yards further on down the hole, getting first out of camera vision and more importantly out of hearing of the players. At this point he reports his position and readiness to report, which is when the Director, if he sees fit, tells the commentator to bring in Clive.

We never now say, 'Are you down there, Clive?' That expression was discarded a very long time ago, but certainly expressions stick and are linked with individuals.

My first efforts as a roving reporter were horrific: it was at the Open Championship at Royal St Georges. It was a last-minute decision by the Director and we were given only minutes to wire up and no time to seek Clive's advice; he was already out there.

There was a delay getting a second set rigged up, but eventually Peter Fitton, who was 'my man', had his pack attached to his back by a harness. From the top of the pack extruded about eight feet of steel aerial and from the bottom a very long length of cable at the end of which was the mike – not the lip type we have in the commentary box, which only picks up sound within inches of it, but an open one which can gather up local sound effects.

Off we went onto the first fairway; Peter suggested we should get well ahead of the match, which was difficult since they were already at their second shots. What I should have done was to take his advice, forget the first hole and move to the second, ignoring the Director's instructions.

As it was, and through no fault of his (for he knew nothing of the delay we had encountered), I could hear in my earphones the Director asking, 'Is Alex out there?'

'Yes,' came my reply.

'No,' whispered Peter into our mike, whispering because we were passing within fifteen yards of Sam Torrance, who had already selected his club for the second shot.

They didn't hear Peter's whisper, and I heard Mark McCormack being told I was down there: 'Alex is down there, he can tell us about Sam's shot.' Sam was now addressing it.

'Cue Alex.' I reached for the mike; my man didn't want to give it to me, he knew the business. I grabbed it and immediately learned why you must be at least fifty yards away and not fifteen. What must be understood is that, with the background noise in the earphones of the production, the cameramen, the static and the spectators, it could be likened to being in a very crowded pub when you think you are talking normally: if everyone else stopped talking suddenly, you would realize that you are actually almost shouting.

'Sam has 150 yards to go.'

Sam, who had covered the first two feet of his backswing, froze; the R&A officials with the match spun round; Tom Watson glared; Sam started towards me. I have never, at any time in my life, felt quite so embarrassed. 'Stop talking,' instructed my Director.

212

I already had; in fact I had made up my mind I would never talk again.

The officials and Sam were bearing down. I held up both my arms like a rugby player caught offside and, promising it wouldn't happen again, made off towards the thick rough, dragging poor Peter with me at the end of my cable, towards the ropes.

Although we were now out of hearing and my breathless assistant was calling me to stop, I ignored him completely. I wanted to get as far away from the first hole as I could. I ducked under the rope and into the gallery.

Seconds later I learned another of Clive's skills, that you don't duck under ropes, you go to the nearest walkway. Oh, you can get under all right, but your sound assistant with his eight-foot aerial cannot, not unless he does as the hapless Fitton did. About nine feet short of the rope he ducked low, and passed beneath it like a lancer. It was when he was safely under and able to stand up that the problem arose.

Our portable mast had passed between the legs of an unsuspecting young lady in an attractive floral dress. As Peter began to straighten up, up went the dress; she shrieked, trying to pull the dress down, at the same time arresting the aerial from doing further damage, which meant poor Peter was unable to gain sufficient head-height to see what was causing the commotion, nor what was stopping his aerial.

Being a pretty strong man, Peter wrenched himself upright and found before him a sight not normally experienced at Open Championships.

That was the first and the only time I have ever seen my companion blush. However, it defused our situation. By now everyone was laughing and we were able to move to the 2nd hole.

By the 8th hole I had been transferred to Raymond Floyd's match. I was keeping well clear of Sam, and was now getting the hang of things; yet even then I was still not in control of my own volume. Being at the far point of the course, the static was creating a huge build-up of noise in the ears, so to make comments I was keeping well away from the players.

Raymond was just bending over his birdie putt when I was brought in. 'If he doesn't allow at least eight inches from the right, he'll miss this.' Fifty yards away, the player hesitated, stepped back, had another look, re-aligned and rapped the ball well to the right. Round it came and dived in.

The crowd cheered, Raymond straightened up, turned to look back up the fairway to where I was standing, raised his hand and called out 'Thank you.' I was shell-shocked. Too many years speaking at functions without microphones, I suppose.

Another of the problems being out there is when you estimate a distance and assess the club the player will use, and move well forward, and particularly on hillocky links, find the ball out of view. Convincing the viewers you are speaking from right alongside the player, you announce he will need a 2 or 3 iron, unable because of the rise in the intervening ground to see that it's a wooden clubhead that is addressing the ball. As the backswing brings the clubhead into view, you realize, too late, that you've committed yet another boob.

46

---•---

MY MISTAKE

Every Christmas the BBC shows its humorous moments where, though sometimes it would appear that Murray Walker practises them, commentators' mistakes are shown for the enjoyment of all, including the commentators. After all, we do get paid when the mistakes are shown abroad and the royalties come back.

I was very lucky to be the one involved when Bernhard Langer climbed the tree on the 17th hole at Fulford. That was shown in so many countries, and the fees were paid.

Whilst it is fun to make a mistake, few in Ireland will forget my friend Roddy Carr's special in the 1988 Irish Open, referring to the Argentine golfer Vicente Fernandez, who walks with a pronounced limp, he proclaimed, 'As a result of a childhood accident, one of Vicente's legs is shorter than the other two!' For you must be able to laugh at yourself or you shouldn't be in television. But one would not wish to make a vulgar or serious mistake: that might prove fatal for the future.

That almost happened to me quite unwittingly, I didn't realize what I had said, or what those in my earphones were laughing at, until much later.

It was my first year and I had arrived from the Open at St Andrews at Sunningdale for the Colgate Ladies, a marvellous tournament that attracted the top women players of the world.

Our commentary box was set by the trees on the far corner of that beautiful downhill dog-leg on the 17th hole. I stood looking at the box for some time before crossing the fairway and going up those steps, thinking how Henry Longhurst used to climb them and how lucky I was now to be doing so.

I went in the door and met the Director.

'Hello, Alex, you'll be sitting here on the right.'

The commentators sit in a row at a bench, with the scorers between us and monitors before us. We have a control switch that, once pushed forward, makes you live to the world. Pulled back it is internal, and in the centre it is dead.

'Clive will be to the left, and Henry Cotton will be between you to answer your questions.'

I had a question already:

'Where's Peter?'

'Peter is in America, he's doing the United States PGA tournament. Harry's in Canada doing the Commonwealth Games.'

'This is it,' I thought. 'A senior man after only one week.'

It was in that week that I learned one of the first lessons in golf commentary, for the BBC's training school that everyone thinks you get sent to is based on the fact that you sink or swim. Listening to and watching your betters is the best training in the world.

What I hadn't realized is that the commentators shouldn't look out of the window, but must watch the monitor.

Common sense would surely suggest that, being thirty or forty feet in the air, and the wall in front of you being glass, you should be taking advantage of the best view. However, if you suggest that a ball has gone where you have seen it go, and no cameraman can, because of his position, get a view of it, that is unprofessional. Better you say, 'I wonder where that one went.'

Often since, I have thought that the box always appears to face due west, so that around 5 p.m., when the action is heating up, the setting sun can shine right through the window onto your monitor so you find yourself squinting into a paler than pale picture and saying 'I think it could be in the bunker' whilst viewers at home, with the 26-inch colour set, the curtains drawn, and the gin and tonic are saying, 'He's as blind as a bat!'

By the third day I hadn't yet learned this lesson and was commentating on the gorgeous Marlene Floyd, who was in the bunker on the far side of the 17th hole, right opposite the box.

I remember suggesting that she mustn't go for the green from the sand, for she was only one shot behind Nancy Lopez. She should play safely to the fairway then go for the green from there. This would keep her in contention. To hit the bunker face and leave the ball in the sand would be disastrous.

As though she heard me, Marlene took a sand wedge and played it out towards the commentary box, a perfect shot.

That would normally be when the Director would tell you to 'stop talking' and take viewers to another hole and bring in Clive.

216

Instead, because everyone on his vast array of screens was walking, he just ordered me to 'talk!'.

In that moment whilst you gather your senses, thinking, 'What shall I say?' the cameraman behind the 17th tee powered up his zoom lens and crashed in on that gorgeous yellow mini-skirted bottom as it wiggled the fifty yards towards the ball; he waited for my next comment.

Had I been looking at my monitor I would have seen this, but I was not, I was looking out of the window.

'Henry Cotton' – I had thought of a point of interest – 'isn't this the finest little hole on the course?'

'Yes indeed,' replied the great man, also looking out of the window, 'but they were all much tighter in my day!'

A story recounted by many and associated with others, but that is how it actually happened.

Another boob occurred on that first season, which was the first year of the Suntory World Match Play. After about fifteen years, Rothmans, who had introduced it, had given up, Colgate tried it for a while and dropped out, then Mark McCormack persuaded a Japanese whisky company to fund it, not so much as a means of advertising their brand, for they hardly sell any in Britain, as to enhance what the company does for the world of sport. Well that's what they tell us.

Being Scottish I wasn't too enamoured of any other country making whisky; nor were the pickets at the gates of Wentworth who, faced with redundancies in Scotland, had travelled down to protest.

I suppose because I must have made my feelings felt, the Directors invited me to join them outside the production caravan, an invitation no one likes to receive.

Once out of earshot they made their point: 'We think we might drop you from this one.' My heart sank; I'd looked forward to my first match play.

'Outside of the Open Championship, this is our biggest event. More people watch this than all the other tournaments.'

'Well, you must need more commentators,' I offered constructively.

'It's your attitude about Japanese whisky.' I spat on the ground.

'There, you see, we can't trust you! You'll come out with something anti-Japanese and cause an uproar.'

'I wouldn't do that, I'm much too professional.' This was my fifth tournament. 'I'd never harm the team, honestly I wouldn't.'

They weakened.

217

'Well, OK, we'll give it a try but just watch your step. If it's cold tomorrow don't you say "There's a NIP in the air today", and we don't want Wentworth called the Burma Road ever again!'

Day One went smoothly then on the second day the new Japanese star Isao Aoki played the young Spanish prodigy Seve Ballesteros, on the day before I presented him with his trophy at the Hilton, and the match went into extra holes. It was getting so dark our cameras were at full-light adjustment when Aoki beat the youngster at the 40th hole of a great match.

The Japanese were delighted; they presented us all with bottles of Suntory whisky. I was delighted, thanking them profusely as my Director looked on.

I believe if I'd as much as cleared my throat at that moment I'd have been out. The BBC were delighted, for we were told that in the small hours of the morning fifty per cent of all Japanese televisions (those in Japan, I mean) were live, their owners watching the BBC's pictures.

What's more, who should get to the final but Aoki. This was dream stuff for the sponsors, and for McCormack, and for the BBC, for it meant Suntory would keep coming, which they have, bringing us some of the year's best viewing at the close of the season.

I was covering the 35th hole, Peter the final hole; mine that wonderful 17th that has featured so much in televised golf. Bill Rogers of America was Aoki's opponent, and both were something like 11 under par for the match and still all-square, without doubt one of the greatest finals ever. Both had driven well; both had played good seconds over the gardens, and the balls lay about fifty yards from the green.

The tension was building; in my earphones linked to 'the scanner' I could judge from the build-up of noise that the Director's were tightening up. So far their show had gone well; only one and a bit more holes to go, not only to finish the match but to end a great year of televised golf for which Slim Wilkinson would later receive an award.

I pushed my red button forward; millions would be listening: 'I think it's Aoki to play first.' A brilliant deduction: it was him.

The Aoki address position is a low crouching one, the toe of his pitching club well off the ground. Our sound crew were picking up his Japanese mutterings as he bobbed up and down, he was definitely trying extra hard. His chattering was quite high-pitched. His old Scottish caddie was nodding in agreement.

The blade struck the ground a fraction short of the ball. It was not going to make the green; it landed short and stopped.

218

'Reaction!' screamed our Director. The cameraman crashed in on the panic-stricken face, then I said it: 'Ah ha, we've gotta wee chink in the armour.'

'You XX!!XX, we knew you'd do it!' The words nearly burst my eardrums; I dropped my mike in shock.

Harry thought this was so funny that throwing his arms up in laughter, he knocked his earpiece out; it fell under his chair.

'Come in, Harry,' said the Director, 'Alex has gone.'

'Anyone seen my earpiece?' asked Harry, completely oblivious of what was going on.

'Harry!'

Harry was searching beneath the bench.

'Come in, Peter! What is going on?' Peter pulled his little red switch back and calmly said, 'S'not my hole, I'm on the 18th!'

'Never mind that, say something!'

Peter pushed the red switch forward; calmly picked up his mike and, using one of his favourite expressions, said, 'Well then, it's nip 'n tuck!'

47

———————•———————

BACK TO THE OFFICE

I had no idea on my arrival at Woburn that it would result in a complete change in direction of my lifestyle. I had always thought how stupid it was that so many golf clubs plough their way through a continual stream of unsatisfactory secretaries and administrators when they often have in their midst an excellent and experienced long-serving professional who would love to help the club: one who knows well the needs of the members and guests of the club, and who, because of a long history of serving the members, understands his position there. Apart from these assets, his knowledge of the game and the financial sense to have survived in the real world of the self-employed complement fully the requirements of club management.

To leave a man possessing such experience out on the cold expanse of the practice ground, or expect him to play a standard of golf which he has long since passed, when he could easily make space for young qualified Assistant Professionals still making their way, instead of bringing him in and utilizing his knowledge, must be stupid.

I am just a little proud of Woburn's Board of Directors, led by the Marquess of Tavistock, who took the unprecedented step of removing me from the Professional's Shop and having the faith to make me the Managing Director of their company, Woburn Golf and Country Club Ltd; their attitude being, that the atmosphere generating from the shop, and the success it was apparently enjoying, were exactly what they wished for from the Club but were not achieving.

There were some who immediately questioned not just the wisdom of this decision but the legality of it. Surely, they claimed, it was unacceptable for a Professional to run an Amateurs' Club, insisting that advice be sought from the Royal and Ancient Golf Club of St Andrews, the home of the amateur game.

The Board of Directors, caught in an embarrassing position, having already offered me the post, immediately asked my permission to ratify their action. I agreed.

Not only did the Royal and Ancient confirm the legality and acceptability of the situation; they congratulated the Board of Directors on being so forward-looking. What was more, they added, the man they had chosen might even stop them losing money and start making some.

This reply delighted Lord Tavistock, who, like his father, the Duke of Bedford, revelled in innovation. However, it distressed some who found the thought of working for a golf Professional too demeaning, and resigned. This also delighted the Marquess.

What has also added to the Board's satisfaction is the growing list of well-known Clubs which have realized that they too have had on their doorstep for years the ideal person for the complex task of running their club and have brought him in from the cold to administer and manage.

A very special reward I enjoyed came recently when spending an afternoon with Lord Tavistock. We were walking on the Duke's course as a part of his recovery to health following his massive brain haemorrhage. As we strolled along the fairways of this beautiful course which he created, we talked of how difficult it was to believe that only twelve years ago it simply hadn't been there; yet now we were rated amongst the very best, and so many of the world's greatest had played it.

He turned to me and made a remark that both touched me deeply and also made me laugh.

'I never thought we would come this far; you and I have made it happen.' He hesitated and then added, 'It's because we have so much in common.'

I stopped and looked at him. 'What on earth could we have in common?' my mind instantly comparing my tenement in Portobello with his Woburn Abbey.

'Well, we both started in a stockbroker's office!'